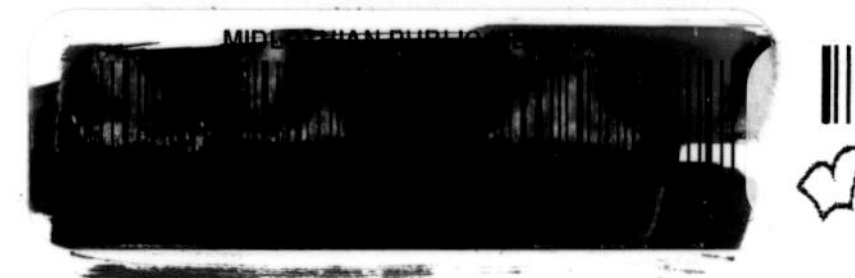

# DISEASES

THE SCIENCE OF THE HUMAN BODY

**BODY SYSTEMS**

**CELLS, TISSUES & ORGANS**

**DISEASES**

**EPIDEMICS & PANDEMICS**

**GENES & GENETICS**

**IMMUNOLOGY**

---

MASON CREST
450 Parkway Drive, Suite D, Broomall, Pennsylvania 19008
(866) MCP-BOOK (toll-free)

James Shoals



First printing
9 8 7 6 5 4 3 2 1

ISBN (hardback) 978-1-4222-4194-3
ISBN (series) 978-1-4222-4191-2
ISBN (ebook) 978-1-4222-7613-6

Cataloging-in-Publication Data on file with the Library of Congress

Developed and Produced by National Highlights Inc.
Interior and cover design: Torque Advertising + Design
Production: Michelle Luke

THE SCIENCE OF THE HUMAN BODY

# DISEASES

JAMES SHOALS

MASON CREST

# KEY ICONS TO LOOK FOR:

**Words to Understand:** These words with their easy-to-understand definitions will increase the reader's understanding of the text while building vocabulary skills.

**Sidebars:** This boxed material within the main text allows readers to build knowledge, gain insights, explore possibilities, and broaden their perspectives by weaving together additional information to provide realistic and holistic perspectives.

**Educational videos:** Readers can view videos by scanning our QR codes, providing them with additional educational content to supplement the text. Examples include news coverage, moments in history, speeches, iconic sports moments, and much more!

**Text-Dependent Questions:** These questions send the reader back to the text for more careful attention to the evidence presented there.

**Research Projects:** Readers are pointed toward areas of further inquiry connected to each chapter. Suggestions are provided for projects that encourage deeper research and analysis.

## QR CODES AND LINKS TO THIRD-PARTY CONTENT

# CONTENTS

# INTRODUCTION

Health is a state of the body in which both, the mind and the body, functions properly and are free from germs. It is a holistic term that includes many different parameters such as physical, social, and mental health. Disease, on the other hand, refers to an abnormal condition affecting the body of an organism. It can affect the working of the entire body or a few organ systems. The surroundings of human beings play a major role in the occurrence of diseases.

## Social Health

Social health is a larger concept and refers to the overall health of a society in which many human beings live together. Both mental and physical health contributes towards a good social health. Thus, social health cannot be achieved in its true sense without achieving good mental and physical health for every individual.

## Physical Health

Physical health refers to the health of the body parts and the body as a whole. The parameters that help to judge whether an individual has a good physical health are height, weight, body mass index, performance during physical activities, and regular medical checkups. A careful insight into one's lifestyle can help in improving one's physical health.

## Mental Health

A human being who is free from all types of mental disorders and has an active mind is said to be mentally healthy. Good mental health is important to lead a normal life. The mental health of an individual can be improved by regular exercise and learning new things.

## Influencing Factors

The health of the body is affected by innumerable factors. A few of these factors include the sleeping patterns, eating habits, type of diet, food hygiene, stress levels, environmental conditions, and genetic inheritance from the parents. In addition, occupational hazards such as exposure to chemicals and radiation can also lead to several health problems.

## Disease-Causing Agents

Diseases are basically of two types—infectious and noninfectious. Diseases that spread from one person to the other are known as infectious diseases while the diseases that do not spread from one person to the other are noninfectious. Microorganisms are small living things that cause diseases and cannot be seen through the naked eye. Various types of microorganisms such as bacteria, fungi, viruses, protozoa, and parasites can cause different diseases in human beings.

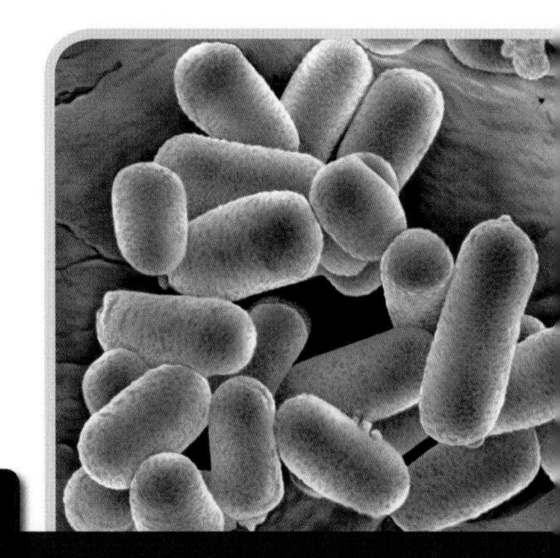

### SIDEBAR: DID YOU KNOW?

- **About 1 in 25 American adults experiences symptoms of serious mental illness in any given year.**
- **Stress can increase the likelihood of developing heart disease, high blood pressure, and irregular heartbeat. That is why doctors call it a "silent killer."**

# AIRBORNE DISEASES

Different disease-causing agents float around in the air. Diseases that can be passed from one person to another through the air are known as airborne diseases. Tiny pathogens are generated while coughing, sneezing, or talking. They can also spread due to contact with saliva or nasal discharges and close mouth-to-mouth contact. Thus, in order to avoid airborne diseases it is important to get vaccinated on time and maintain a healthy immune system.

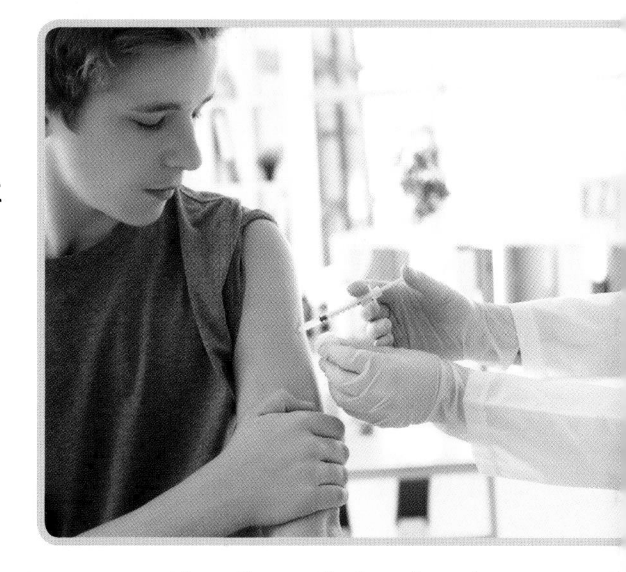

## Chicken Pox

Chicken pox (varicella) is an airborne viral disease. The disease spreads through the sneezing and coughing of the infected individual. (It can also spread via physical contact with the watery secretion from the rashes.) The viral infection leads to the formation of several red, fluid-filled blisters on the skin. The viral infections cannot be treated with antibiotics and tend to clear up on their own in a few days. An oatmeal bath in lukewarm water can help reduce the itching. The varicella vaccine is very effective in preventing the illness.

## WORDS TO UNDERSTAND

pathogen: a microorganism that can cause disease.

respiratory: having to do with breathing.

viral: describes a condition caused by viruses.

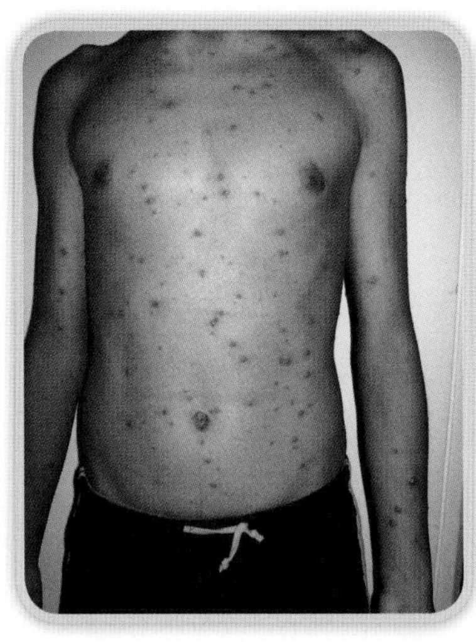

## Measles

Measles (rubella) is a highly contagious viral disease that spreads through the respiratory droplets of an infected person. The onset of the disease usually begins with a high fever, cough, and runny nose. These symptoms are followed by the occurrence of red rashes that develop after a few days. Usually they begin on the forehead and then appear around the rest of the body. It takes about two weeks to recover from the measles. Measles is pretty rare in the United States because there is a very effective vaccine against the disease. Vaccination doesn't just protect individuals; it protects an entire community. Measles is extremely dangerous to pregnant women, because it can hurt or kill their developing babies. That's why it's important for the entire community to maintain high rates of vaccination, so that measles doesn't spread.

## Mumps

Another common viral airborne disease is mumps. The disease is spread through respiratory droplets and leads to pain and swelling in the salivary glands. The common symptoms of the infection include facial pain, fever, sore throat, and swelling of the jaws. There are fewer than 20,000 cases a year in the United States because most people are vaccinated. The disease cannot be cured, but measures such as warm water gargles and eating soft foods can help ease symptoms. Most people get better in a few weeks.

## Influenza

Influenza, or flu, is the viral infection of the respiratory system that is caused by many different types of viruses. The symptoms of the disease are headache, chilling sensation, cough, sore throat, and body ache. The disease can be deadly for newborn babies, elderly people, and people with a weak immune system.

## Anthrax

Anthrax is an infectious airborne disease caused by bacteria. The spores of the bacteria are present in the air and enter the body when inhaled or via open cuts or sores. The anthrax bacteria can also infect human beings through contact with the skin and hairs of animals such as sheep and goats. The bacterial infection usually leads to skin and lung diseases. Anthrax can be treated by the use of antibiotics and can be prevented by vaccination.

Find out more about measles.

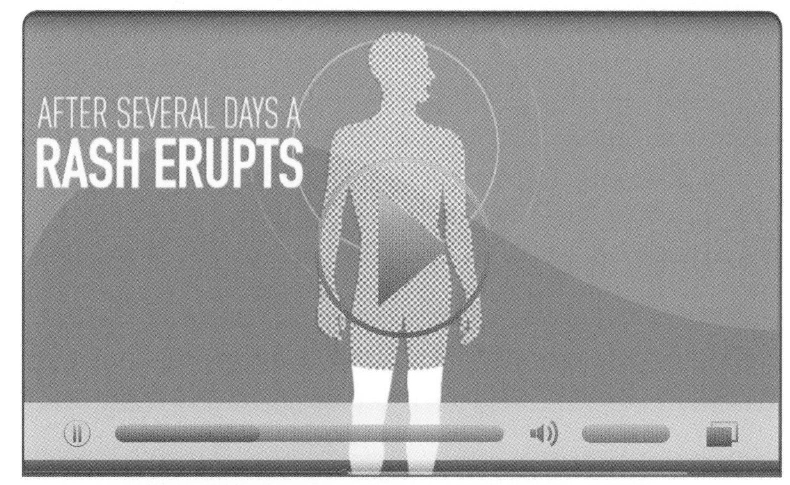

### SIDEBAR: DID YOU KNOW?

- During World War I, a large number of soldiers were hospitalized due to mumps.
- About three million people in the United States got chicken pox every year before its vaccine was invented.

# WATERBORNE DISEASES

Waterborne diseases spread through water that is contaminated with microorganisms. The contamination of water can occur for many reasons, such as accidental mixing of harmful substances in water, fecal contamination of water, improper cleaning, and so on. Most waterborne diseases are not fatal, but they are extremely unpleasant.  But proper care, hygiene practices, and vaccination should be followed to avoid the occurrences of waterborne diseases.

## Cholera

Cholera is a bacterial waterborne disease that is spread by drinking contaminated water. The bacteria release a toxin in the body that leads to the production of excessive water in the small intestine. The common symptoms of cholera are severe pain in the abdomen, watery diarrhea, excessive thirst, and lack of tears. The disease commonly occurs during times of flood, famine, and in places that have poor hygiene.

## Hepatitis A and E

Hepatitis A and hepatitis E are two common waterborne diseases, although you can also get them through contact with someone who is already infected. These diseases spread through water that is

### WORDS TO UNDERSTAND

hygiene: cleanliness.
intravenous: through the veins.
jaundice: a condition involving yellowing of the skin and the whites of the eyes.
toxin: a poisonous substance.

contaminated with fecal matter or through poor hygiene practices. The main causative agents of both types of hepatitis are viruses. The viral infection leads to symptoms such as swelling of the liver, dark-colored urine and stools, loss of appetite, and jaundice. The disease can be cured by the use of antibiotics.

## Typhoid Fever

Typhoid fever is a waterborne disease caused by bacteria. After ingestion, the bacteria can easily spread to the intestine, blood stream spleen, liver, and gallbladder. The symptoms of the disease develop after 7 to 21 days of infection, causing severe constipation or diarrhea, fever, red-colored spots on the chest, and enlarged spleen and liver. The disease can be cured by use of intravenous body fluids and antibiotics.

## Dysentery

Dysentery is another common disease that is spread through the consumption of contaminated food and water. It affects a part of the intestine, causing severe diarrhea. The infection can be caused by bacteria or intestinal parasites. Dysentery is also known as "bloody diarrhea" because the loose, watery stools contain blood. The disease can be cured with proper medication and administration of intravenous fluids.

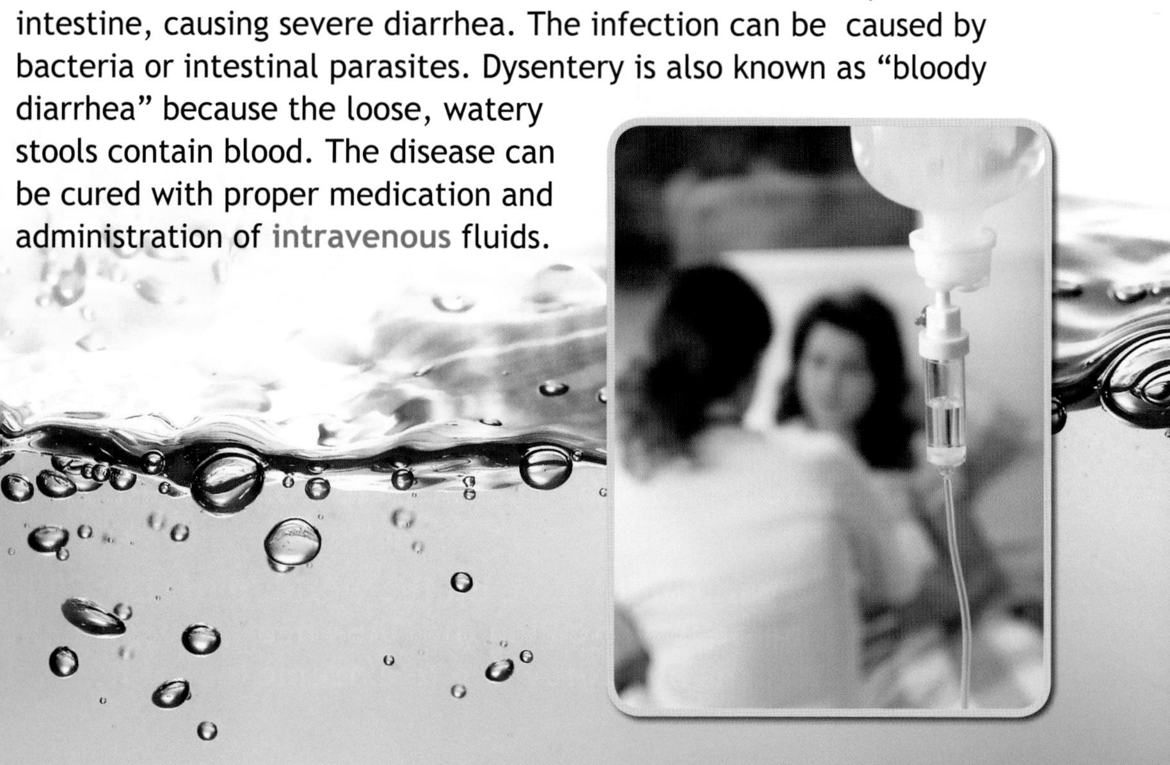

## Worm Diseases

Worm diseases are another type of waterborne diseases that are caused by flatworms and round worms. These diseases usually spread by the consumption of undercooked beef, pork, and by the consumption of water contaminated with the eggs of worms. The infection by the worms usually occurs in the small and large intestine. The worms can live in the body for years. The common symptoms of worm diseases include coughing, worms in stool, and stomach pain. The diseases can be cured with the use of different medicines.

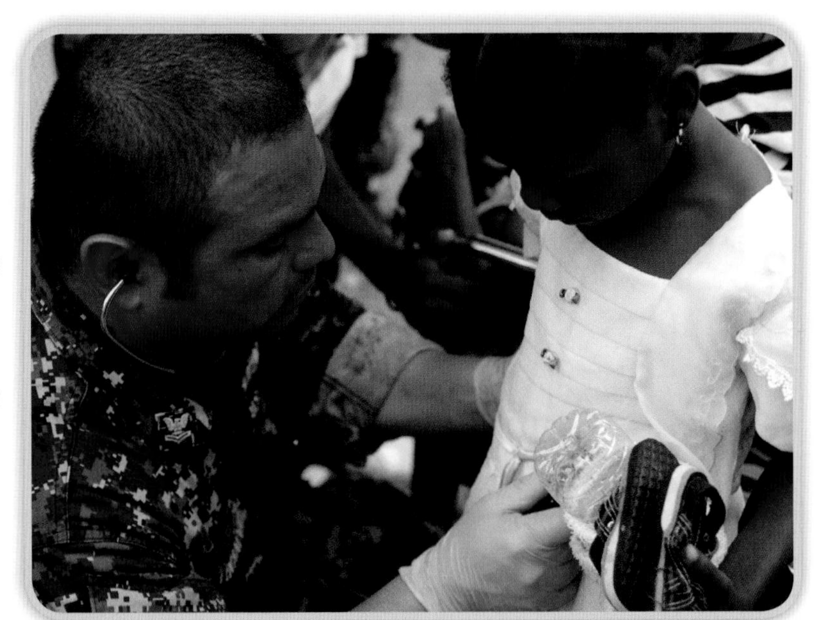

### SIDEBAR: DID YOU KNOW?

- **Regular hand-washing, especially before eating and after going to bathroom, can keep people safe from hepatitis A and dysentery.**
- **Seven cholera pandemics have hit the world in the last 200 years. This disease is also called the "blue death" because the patient's skin turns blue-grey due to extreme loss of fluids.**

# VECTOR-BORNE DISEASES

Vector-borne diseases are diseases that are spread through vectors such as bacteria, fungi, viruses, protozoa, and parasites. Flies, ticks, bats, rats, and dogs can also act as vectors for transmission of different diseases. Thus, in order to prevent vector-borne diseases precautionary measures such as vaccinations, mosquito repellents, and mosquito nets should be used.

## Sleeping Sickness

Sleeping sickness is a parasitic vector-borne disease. The parasite is carried by tsetse flies in rural areas of Africa. The parasite enters the body through the insect bite and multiplies in the blood stream. The disease causes excessive drowsiness, swelling of the brain, insomnia, anxiety, sand wollen, red nodules at the site of the insect bite. It can be cured with the help of several different medicines.

### WORDS TO UNDERSTAND

hydrophobia: extreme fear of water.

parasitic: relating to parasites, which are organisms that depend on another organism for survival.

prevalent: widespread.

preventive: protective; an action that keeps something else from occurring.

vector: a living or non-living agent that carries the disease.

## Yellow Fever

Yellow fever is a viral fever that is spread through the Aedes mosquito in tropical areas. The disease is so-named due to one of the symptoms: jaundice, which turns the skin yellow. The infection also causes high fever and chills, nausea, muscle pains, headache, and black vomiting. There is no known cure for the disease, so preventive measures (like insect repellent) and vaccination must be used.

## Malaria

Malaria is another common vector-borne fever. It spreads through the bite of the female Anopheles mosquito. The insect bite transfers the parasites to the blood stream. In addition to fever, the infection causes severe chills, vomiting, jaundice, and diarrhea. Malaria is a very serious illness but it can be treated with proper medication.

*Anopheles mosquito*

## Dengue

Dengue is a type of infectious vector-borne disease. The disease is caused due to a virus that enters the body through the bite of Aedes mosquito. The infected person suffers from high fever, headache, joint pain, and vomiting.

*Aedes mosquito*

Dengue can be life-threatening and thus immediate medical help is required to treat the disease.

## Japanese Encephalitis

A viral disease which affects human beings and animals is Japanese encephalitis (JE). The virus is carried by the Culex mosquito and causes inflammation of the parts of the brain on entering the body. The symptoms of the disease may be mild or severe causing fever headache, stiffness in the neck, seizures, coma and even death. Vaccination is a good measure to prevent the disease as no specific treatment is available for JE.

*Culex mosquito*

## Rabies

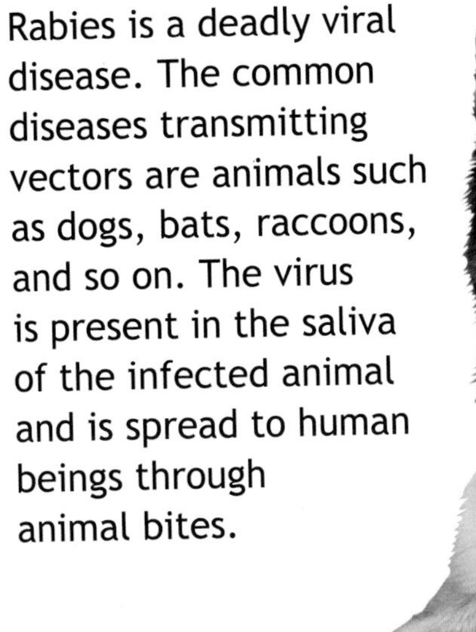

Rabies is a deadly viral disease. The common diseases transmitting vectors are animals such as dogs, bats, raccoons, and so on. The virus is present in the saliva of the infected animal and is spread to human beings through animal bites.

The symptoms of the disease include fever, fatigue, headache, hallucination, hydrophobia, and paralysis. In case of animal bites, immediate medical help should be taken as any delay can lead to the death of the individual. Rabies vaccination also helps in preventing the disease.

This video details global efforts to combat malaria.

## SIDEBAR: DID YOU KNOW?

- The rabies vaccine was invented by Louis Pasteur, a French scientist, in 1885.
- Yellow fever is most prevalent in Africa and America.

# DIGESTIVE SYSTEM DISORDERS

The digestive system is an important part of the body, made up of several organs such as the stomach, pancreas, liver, and intestines. The system converts the food that we eat into useful energy for the body. The digestive system is affected by several common diseases and disorders, a few of which are mentioned below.

## Heartburn

A digestive system problem affecting the stomach and the food pipe is heartburn. Heartburn, or acidity, is caused due to the upward flow of the acid which is produced in the stomach. This acid enters the food pipe and causes irritation of the food pipe, a burning sensation, and chest pain. Avoiding hot and spicy foods can help in controlling the heartburn.

## Indigestion

Indigestion, also called dyspepsia, is another common problem of the digestive system. Indigestion can be caused by

## WORDS TO UNDERSTAND

**enzyme:** a substance produced by the body that sparks a particular reaction.

**intolerance:** here, the inability to eat a particular food without experiencing an unpleasant physical reaction.

**pancreas:** a gland near the stomach that secretes digestive enzymes.

minor problems like overeating, or more serious problems such as stomach ulcers, and cancer. The common symptoms of dyspepsia include a constant feeling of full stomach, nausea, vomiting, and pain in the upper abdomen. Mild indigestion can be cured by properly chewing the food, eating low-fat meals, and avoiding carbonated drinks, coffee, and smoking.

## Stomach Ulcer

Lesions or sores occurring on the inner lining of the stomach are known as stomach, or gastric, ulcers. The ulcers in the stomach may be caused due to bacterial infection or due to an increased amount of stomach acids. Changes in color of the stools, stomach pain, nausea, and heartburn— are some of the common symptoms of stomach ulcers. Ulcers need medication to heal.

## Constipation

Constipation is another very common intestinal problem. It is characterized by the occurrence of hard and dry stools. Solid stools are produced due to excessive absorption of water from the intestine. Abdominal cramps and pain are symptoms of constipation. Frequently drinking water and eating fiber-rich diet help ease the problem.

## Gallstones

A gallstone is a medical condition which affects the gall bladder of the digestive system. Gallstones are hard deposits of the digestive juices that are produced in the gall bladder. The stones can cause stomach pain, nausea, and vomiting.

## Lactose Intolerance

Lactose intolerance is the inability of an individual to digest milk and milk products properly. Milk is made up of a sugar, lactose. Lactose intolerance arises when the body produces insufficient amounts of lactase, an enzyme required to break down lactose. The undigested milk may cause stomach pain, gas, and diarrhea. It is a very common disorder that can affect people of all age groups. Fortunately the disorder does not lead to serious consequences and improves if dairy products are simply avoided.

### SIDEBAR: DID YOU KNOW?

- Avoidance of dairy products by lactose-intolerant people can cause a deficiency of vitamin D.
- The digestive system depends on muscles to move food through the body, not gravity. That's why you can still digest food when you're lying down. In fact, you could even digest food if you were upside down!

# HEART AND BLOOD DISORDERS

The heart and blood are part of the circulatory system. The heart pumps oxygen-rich blood to the body. Blood is comprised of red blood cells, white blood cells, platelets, and plasma. All these cells perform different functions such as carrying oxygen to different body parts and fighting infections. However, an unhealthy diet, diabetes, obesity, and smoking can lead to certain heart and blood diseases.

## Blood Pressure

The pressure applied by the moving blood on the walls of the blood vessels is known as the blood pressure. Blood pressures lower than normal or higher than normal are a cause of problem for people. People suffering from blood pressure problems feel a lack of concentration, blurred vision, tiredness, and depression. Eating a healthy, low-fat diet and exercising properly help in maintaining a proper blood pressure.

## WORDS TO UNDERSTAND

**arteries:** muscular tubes that convey blood to and from the heart and around the body.

**palpitations:** noticeably rapid or irregular heartbeat.

**platelets:** components of blood that assist with clotting.

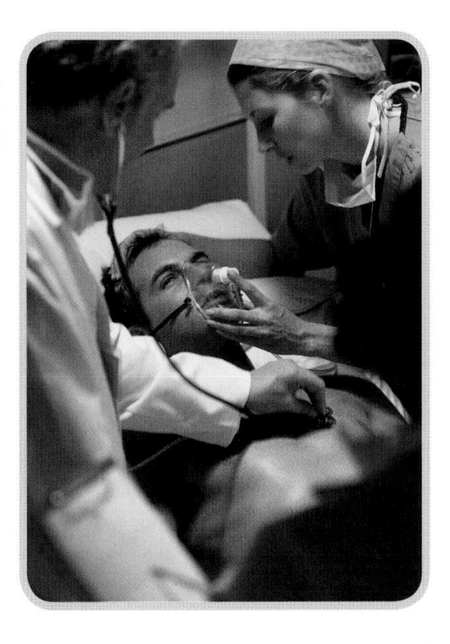

## Angina

Angina is not a heart disease or a disorder but is a common symptom of heart disease. Angina, or a pain in the chest, arises due to the blockage of the arteries of the heart. This blockage causes a lack of blood flow and fresh oxygen to the heart. A doctor should be consulted in cases of chest pain.

## Heart Attack

Heart attack is a resulting condition of a heart disease. A heart attack occurs due to a sudden obstruction in the blood flow to a part of the heart. The symptoms of a heart attack include prolonged chest pain, pressure in the chest, heavy sweating, palpitations, cough, and fainting. A doctor should be consulted immediately in cases of symptoms of a heart attack. Some patients can be cured by medications while in some cases doctors may perform coronary bypass surgery.

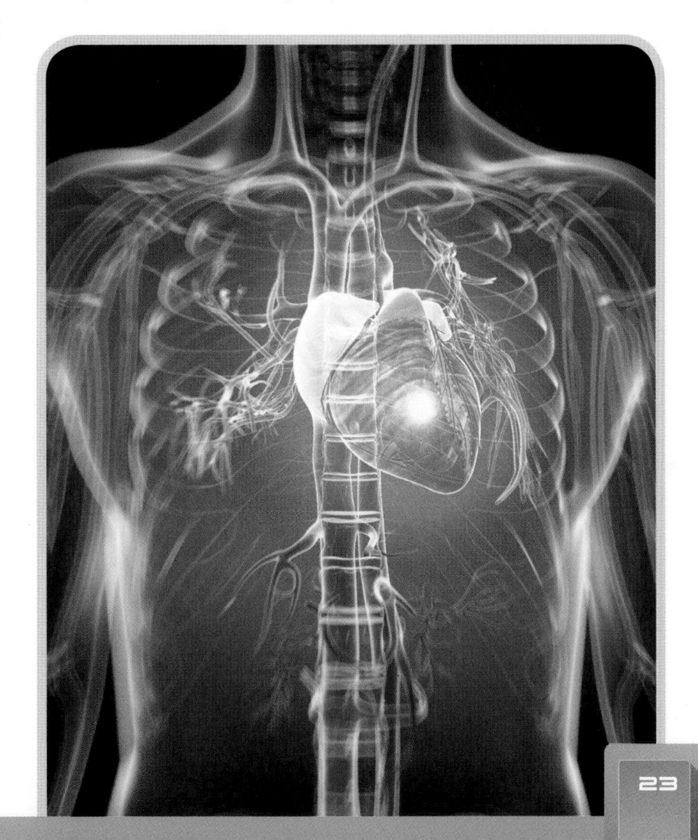

## Heart Failure

Heart failure is a disorder in which the heart is unable to supply enough blood to the body parts. Swollen legs, fatigue, angina, loss of appetite, and abnormal weight loss or gain are a few indications of heart failure.

## Anemia

Anemia is a common type of blood disorder—that involves a lack of red blood cells. As a result, oxygen is less available in the body and the person feels pale, weak, gets headache and has difficulty concentrating. There are numerous types of anemia, some mild and some serious.  Eating an iron- and vitamin-rich diet can help avoid anemia.

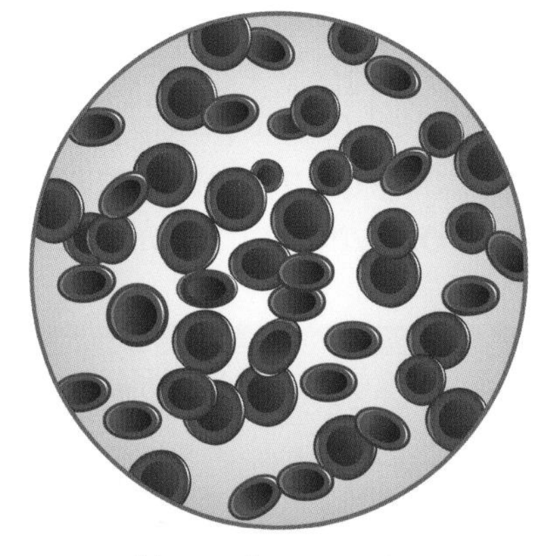

Normal amount of red blood cells

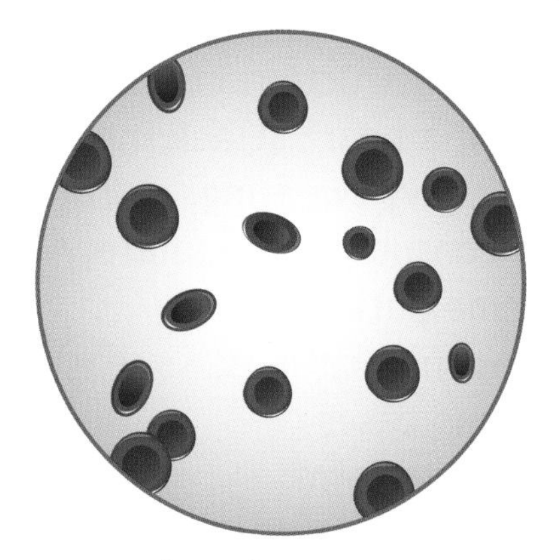

Anemic amount of red blood cells

### SIDEBAR: DID YOU KNOW?

- Women under age 50 are two times as likely to die of a heart attack than men of the same age.
- People with high blood pressure are more susceptible to heart attacks, strokes, and kidney failures.

# DISEASES OF THE RESPIRATORY SYSTEM

The nose, trachea, bronchi, chest cavity, lungs, and diaphragm together form the respiratory system of the body. The primary function of the respiratory system is to provide the body with oxygen.

The air that we breathe is made up of many gases, dust particles, and microorganisms. When inhaled, the components can sometimes harm the respiratory system, leading to various types of infections and diseases.

## Common Cold

The common cold is one of the most common types of respiratory infection. It occurs due to viral infection in the upper respiratory tract. The most common symptoms of common cold include an increase in body temperature, headache, cough, sore throat, sneezing, and a runny nose. With rest and fluids, colds will usually resolve on their own within a few days.

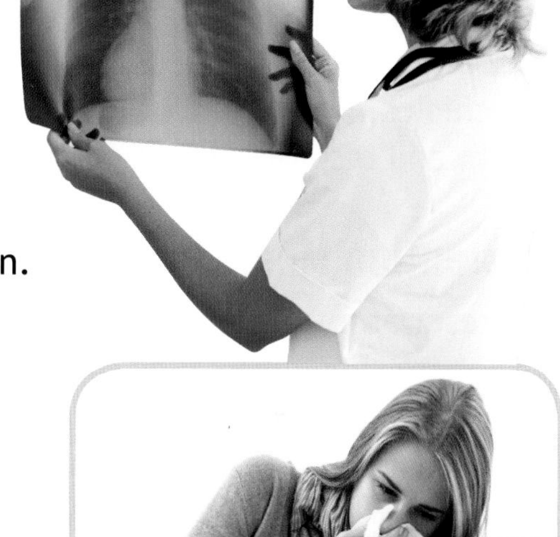

### WORDS TO UNDERSTAND

bronchi: tubes that branch off from the trachea and carry oxygen deeper into the lungs.

diaphragm: a muscle just above the stomach.

trachea: the windpipe.

## Tonsillitis

The tonsils are tissues in the throat that filter the bacteria and viruses that are inhaled through the mouth and the nose. Tonsillitis is a common throat problem that causes severe throat pain, problems in swallowing, fever, and bad breath. Tonsillitis can be cured by the use of antibiotics and warm water gurgles.

## Bronchitis

Bronchitis is an inflammation of the mucous membrane in the bronchi. It takes two forms: acute and chronic. The acute form is caused by bacterial infection and tends to follow other respiratory infections. It usually results in a reduction of the lumen of the bronchi and bronchioles, production of heavy clogging mucus with debilitating cough, and respiratory difficulty.

## Prevention Measures

The respiratory system is very important for the survival of an organism. Thus, care should be taken in order to prevent the occurrence of respiratory diseases. The face and nose should be covered with a mask in places of high air pollution and dust. Quit smoking and be very careful if working with heavy metals and gases.

## Asthma

Asthma is a respiratory disease of the air tubes, or bronchi. Whenever any foreign particle enters the air tubes, they swell up, reducing the air flow. This situation may lead to severe coughing, suffocation, wheezing, and breathing problems. Asthma can be mild or severe. It is fairly common in children, but some will outgrow it as adults.

People with asthma should try to avoid substances or situations that trigger their attacks, and always have a plan ready of what to do if an attack occurs.

## Tuberculosis

Tuberculosis (TB) is another infectious disease of the respiratory system. It is a slow-spreading disease caused by a bacteria. The bacterial infection begins in the lungs but can spread to other parts of the body. A persistent cough, weakness, fever, chills, and weight loss are a few symptoms associated with TB. The disease is curable but it requires proper care and treatment, which may require multiple medications. People with HIV/AIDS must be especially careful when it comes to TB, because their compromised immune systems make them highly susceptible.

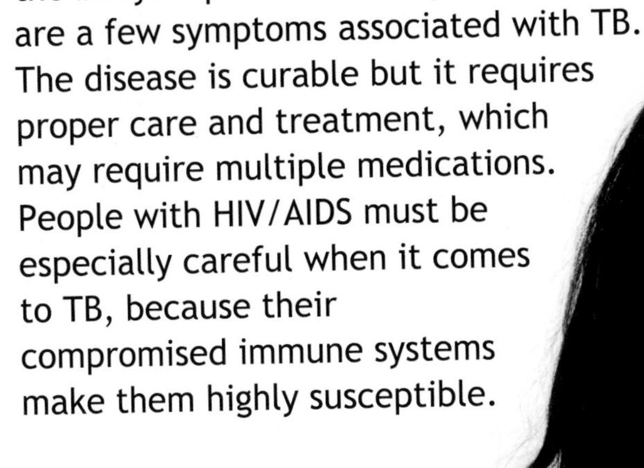

### SIDEBAR: DID YOU KNOW?

- Chronic bronchitis can last from several months to years.
- Tonsillitis can spread by using and infected person's toothbrush, cups, or other utensils.

# NERVOUS SYSTEM DISORDERS

The nervous system is the body's control-and-coordination system. It comprises of the brain, spinal cord, and many different types of nerves that are spread throughout the body. Thus, any type of disorder or disease in the nervous system can lead to non-functionality in any part of the body. Nervous system diseases can occur because of a trauma, injury, developmental disorders, and genetic errors, and are degenerative in nature. Regular exercise and a healthy diet can help in maintaining a healthy nervous system.

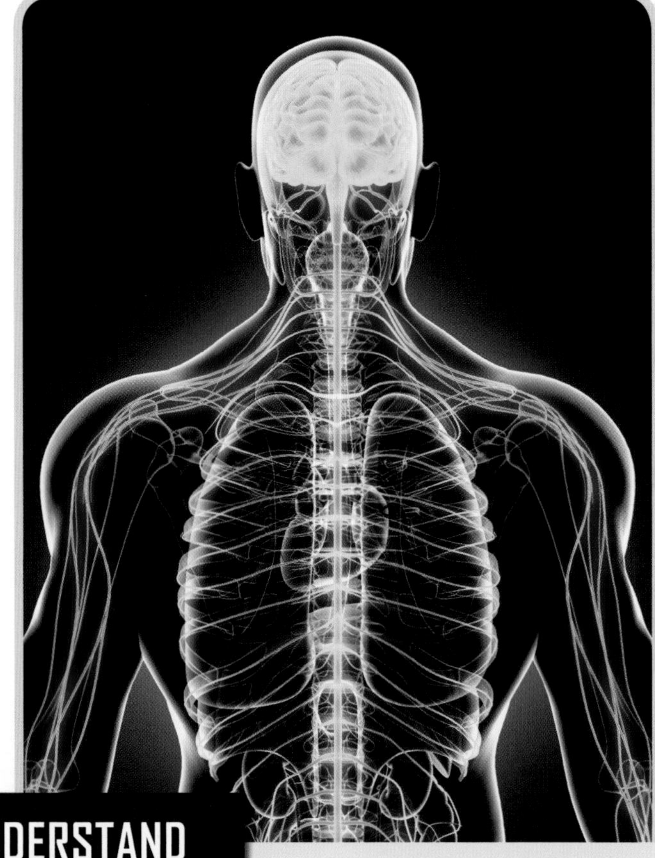

## Spondylosis

Spondylosis is a common degenerative disease of the backbone. It is caused

## WORDS TO UNDERSTAND

clot: here, a clump of blood cells that can cause problems as it travels through the body.

degenerative: describes a condition that gets worse over time.

seizure: a convulsion caused by electrical activity in the brain.

by the normal wear and tear of the joints and tissues. It can affect any region of the spine—upper, middle, and lower. The occurrence of spondylosis is marked by a loss of sensation in the arms, legs, and shoulders, sudden numbness, and loss of balance.

## Stroke

A stroke is a condition of the brain in which a clot causes the stoppage of blood flow. It causes numbness in different parts of the body, loss of coordination, and improper body functioning.

## Alzheimer's Disease

Alzheimer's disease is a degenerative disease of the brain and nervous system. It usually occurs in older people. The disease progresses slowly, leading to a gradual loss of memory and thinking ability. The affected individual may also have problems with decision-making, judgment, and behavior.

## Slipped Disk

A slipped disk is another disorder of the lower backbone. In this medical condition, a disk present between the bones of the spinal cord dislocates from its place and causes severe back pain. A person suffering from a slipped disk may also experience numbness, burning sensation, and weakness.

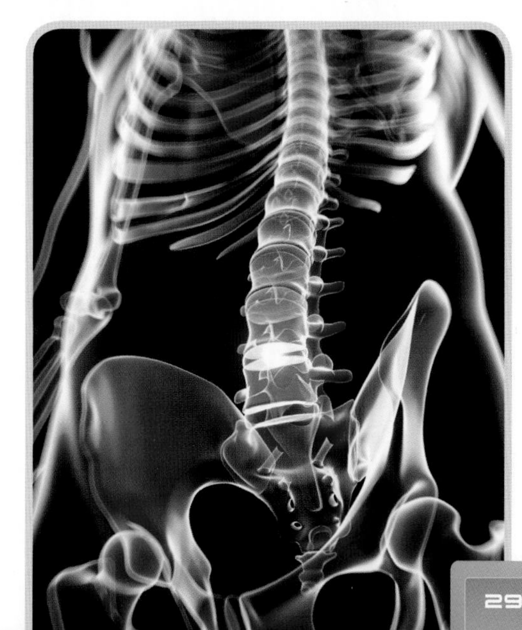

## Epilepsy

Epilepsy is a brain disorder characterized by regular seizures. A seizure is a small period during which brain activity reduces and the brain does not work properly. Several reasons such as brain injury, heart attack, birth defects, and other diseases may lead to epilepsy.

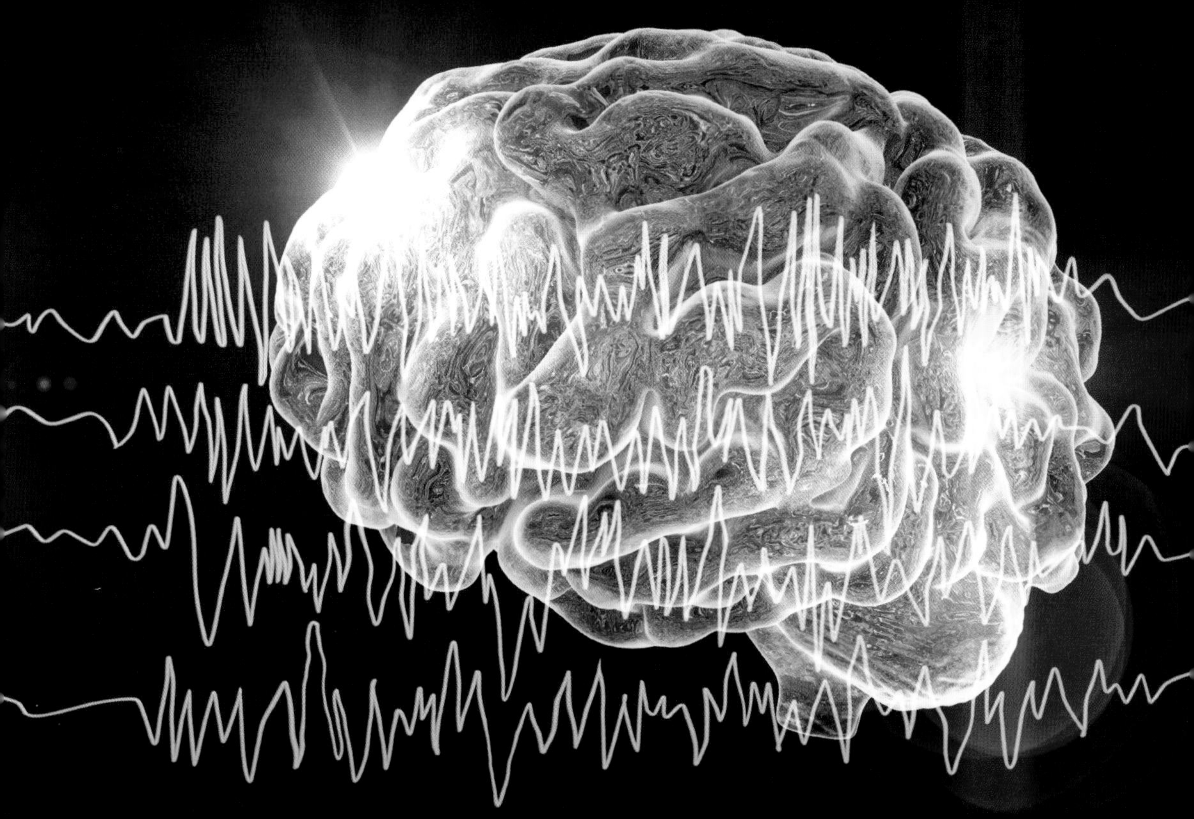

### SIDEBAR: DID YOU KNOW?

- More than 5 million Americans suffer from Alzheimer's disease. That number may triple by 2050.
- Damage in the left side of the brain due to stroke may result in paralysis of the right side of the body and vice versa.

# EYE AND EAR PROBLEMS

We understand the world around us with help of the sense organs. These are extremely sensitive organs and are easily affected by different disorders. The most extreme problems are blindness and deafness. People can be blind or deaf at birth or become so later in life, due to some other ailment.

## Color Blindness

Color blindness is an incurable defect of the eye. A color-blind individual cannot see some or all the colors that other normal individuals can see. Color blindness arises due to the absence of color granules in the cone cells of the eye. The Ishihara test is commonly used to test color blindness.

## Far- and Nearsightedness

Farsightedness and nearsightedness are common vision problems. People who are farsighted (hyperopic) can see faraway things well but have trouble close up, while nearsighted (myopic) people are the reverse.  The light is either focused in front of the retina as in

## WORDS TO UNDERSTAND

Ishihara test: a color perception test.
middle ear: the part of the ear that transmits sound waves to the ear drum.
progressive: here, a disease that slowly gets worse.

nearsightedness or behind the retina as in farsightedness. Both types of eye defects can be managed by wearing eye glasses or contact lenses. Often they can also be corrected permanently through laser surgery.

## Ear Infection

Otitis media or ear infection is a type of infection of the middle ear. The infection is characterized by the presence of fluid and mucus in the tubes. The condition is painful and reduces the person's ability to hear. This type of infection is quite common in young children. It's usually not serious but should be addressed with a doctor so that no permanent damage occurs.

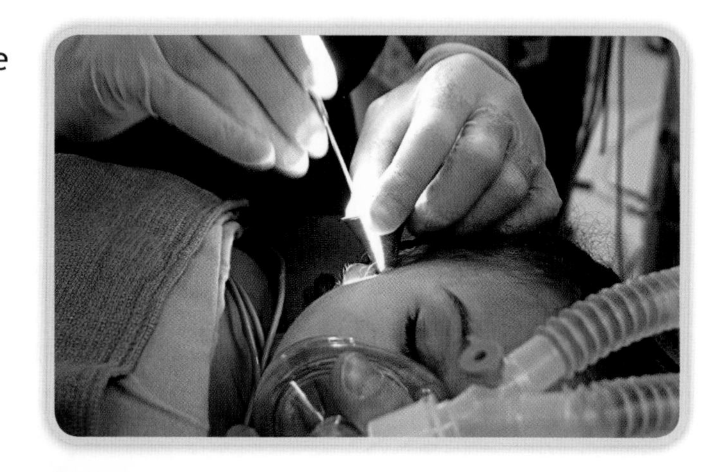

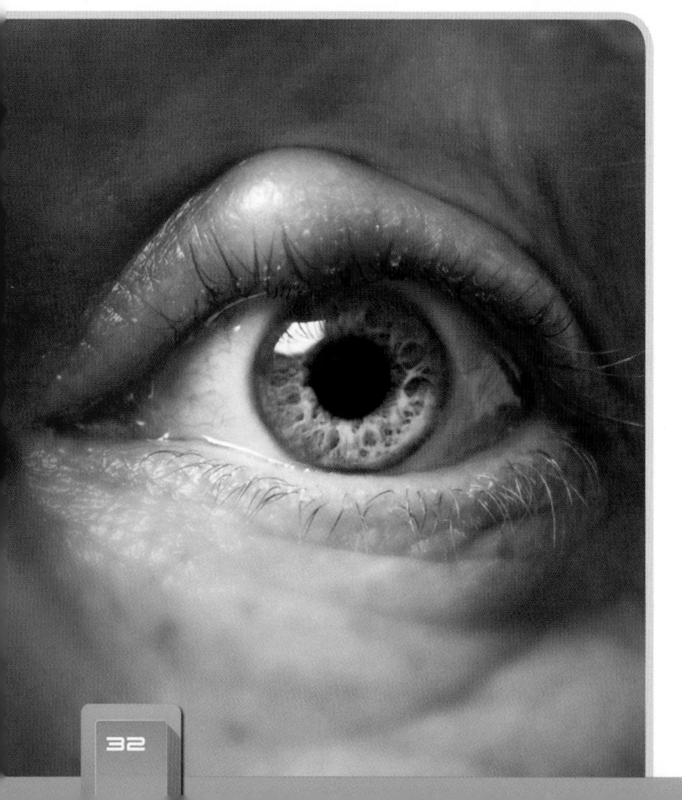

## Sty

A sty is an infection of the eyelids. The bacterial infection leads to the blockage of the secretionary glands on the eyelids. It can form on the outer or inner side of the eyelid and remains swollen and painful. Stress, overuse of cosmetics, poor hygiene can lead to the occurrence of a sty. It does not lead to a serious infection but timely care and medication is necessary.

## Ear Wax

Ear wax, or cerumen, is an oily and waxy substance that is produced in the ear canal. It is produced by the oil glands of the ear and is very useful. It helps in trapping the sweat, dust, foreign particles, and bacteria that enter the ear. With time the ear wax hardens and may fall out of the ear on its own.

## Pink Eye

Pink eye, or conjunctivitis, is a common communicable eye disease that causes itching and burning. The common causes of pink eye are bacterial infection, allergies, and irritants such as gaseous fumes, certain eye-care products, and contact lenses. The eyes should not be rubbed and must be washed with water regularly.

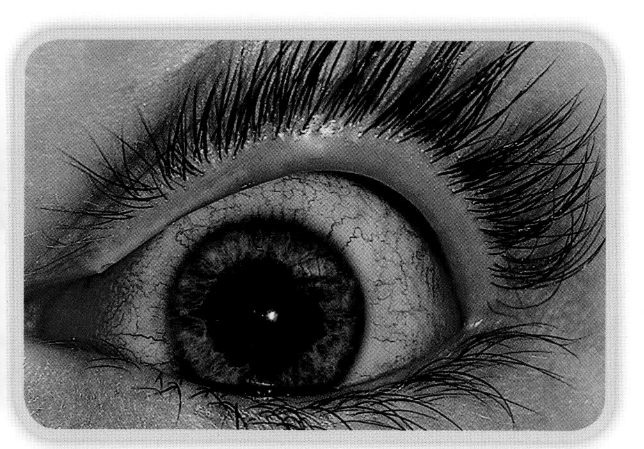

## Cataract

A cataract is an eye condition in which the eye lens becomes clouded due to protein deposits. This condition commonly affects elderly people.

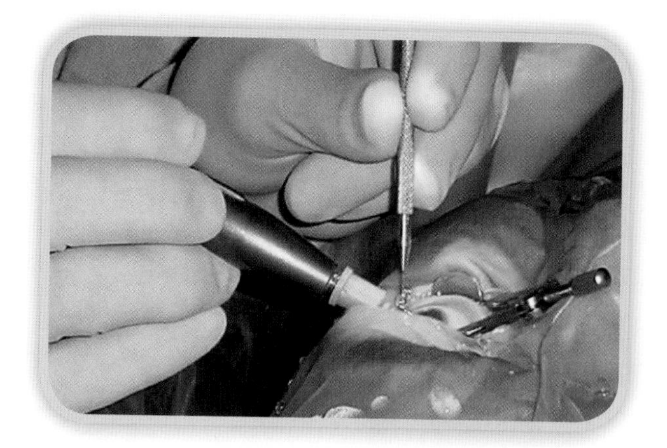

The condition leads to hampered vision and reduced color visibility. It is a progressive disease and may lead to blindness. Surgery is the most effective treatment of cataract.

A video about what it's like to be color blind.

## SIDEBAR: DID YOU KNOW?

- It is a myth that wearing glasses makes vision worse over time. It's also not true that you should wear weak glasses to make your eyes "work harder." That will not help your vision—instead, you should wear the glasses that help you see as well as possible.
- Some people suffer from a rare form of color blindness called unilateral dichromacy which means one of their eyes is normal sighted and one is color blind.

# ORAL DISEASES

The tongue, mouth, salivary glands together with their associated organs form part of the digestive system. The entire oral cavity is very sensitive to the attack of diseases. The oral diseases are basically of three types—tooth diseases, gum diseases, and oral cancer.

## Tartar and Plaque

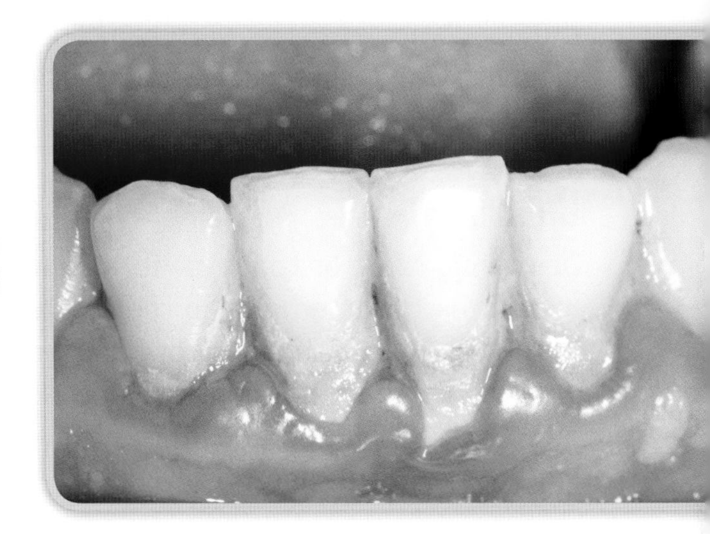

Plaque is a deposit of bacteria on the surface of the teeth, which appears as a white film. If not removed, the plaque can harden, become yellowish, and settle on the tooth to form tartar. The tartar is formed at the base of teeth where the teeth meet the gums.

## Wisdom Teeth

Wisdom teeth refer to a set of four molar teeth. These teeth are very deep-rooted and arise between the ages of 17-25 years. A human being may develop all four, fewer than four, or none at all. The arrival of a wisdom tooth can be extremely painful and a dentist must always be consulted for its proper care.

## WORDS TO UNDERSTAND

**insomnia:** a chronic inability to fall asleep or stay asleep.

**oral cavity:** refers to the mouth, lips, teeth, tongue, and tissues.

**salivary glands:** glands in the mouth that produce saliva, which moistens food and starts the process of digestion.

## Gingivitis

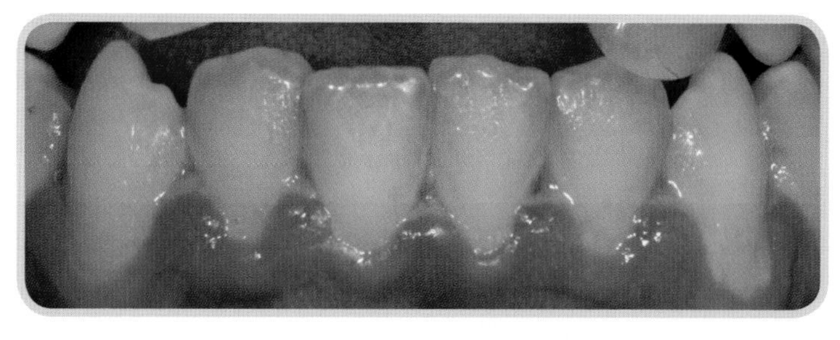

Gingivitis is a common gum disease in which the gums become red and swell up. The major cause of gingivitis is plaque and tartar. The bacteria infect the gums and they become sensitive, turn red, and even bleed. Other than this gingivitis can also occur due to poor dental hygiene, poorly fitting mouth devices, and brushing very hard.

## Cavities

Dental cavities, or tooth cavity, is another widespread problem of the teeth. Cavities in the teeth occur because of bacterial growth. The bacteria convert food remains into acid, which degrades the teeth. This can lead to the formation of a cavity.

## Mouth Ulcers

Mouth ulcers are open sores in the mouth that are red in color, swollen, and often painful. Ulcers can occur in any part of the mouth including the cheek walls, tongue, and hard or soft palate. Several causes such as gingivitis, other oral problems, hot food items, and poor oral hygiene can initiate mouth ulcers.

## Preventive Measures

In order to avoid the onset of oral problems, good oral hygiene should be maintained. This can be done by eating fewer sweets, brushing slowly and twice daily, and using dental floss regularly. However, a dentist must be consulted in case of tartar formation, gingivitis, and ulcers.

## Teeth Grinding

Bruxism, or teeth grinding, is the act of sliding the teeth against each other or tightly clenching the jaws. People may clench their teeth consciously during the daytime or unconsciously while asleep. It can lead to a pain in the jaws and teeth, teeth sensitivity, and **insomnia**.

## Thrush

Thrush is a fungal infection of the mouth and the tongue. The fungus is always present in the mouth but causes infection only when the body is weak. The condition leads to the development of white sores and lesions in the mouth. The disease commonly occurs in infants and usually improves on its own without any treatment.

### SIDEBAR: DID YOU KNOW?

- Snacking on celery, carrots, and apples helps in clearing away the food sticking to teeth.
- Carbonated beverages are a significant cause of cavities in teenagers.

# SKIN DISEASES

Skin is the multilayered organ of touch and sensation. It is made up of three layers, each of which performs a different function. The hairs and nails are also a part of the skin and are made up of proteins. The skin helps us to respond to our surroundings. Since the skin is the covering of the human body, it can be affected by many disease-causing agents.

## Acne

Acne is a common skin problem. It usually emerges during adolescence. It occurs in the form of small whiteheads and blackheads on the face, neck, and chest region. Hormonal changes in the body are a main cause of acne. Maintaining good personal hygiene helps in reducing the problem of acne.

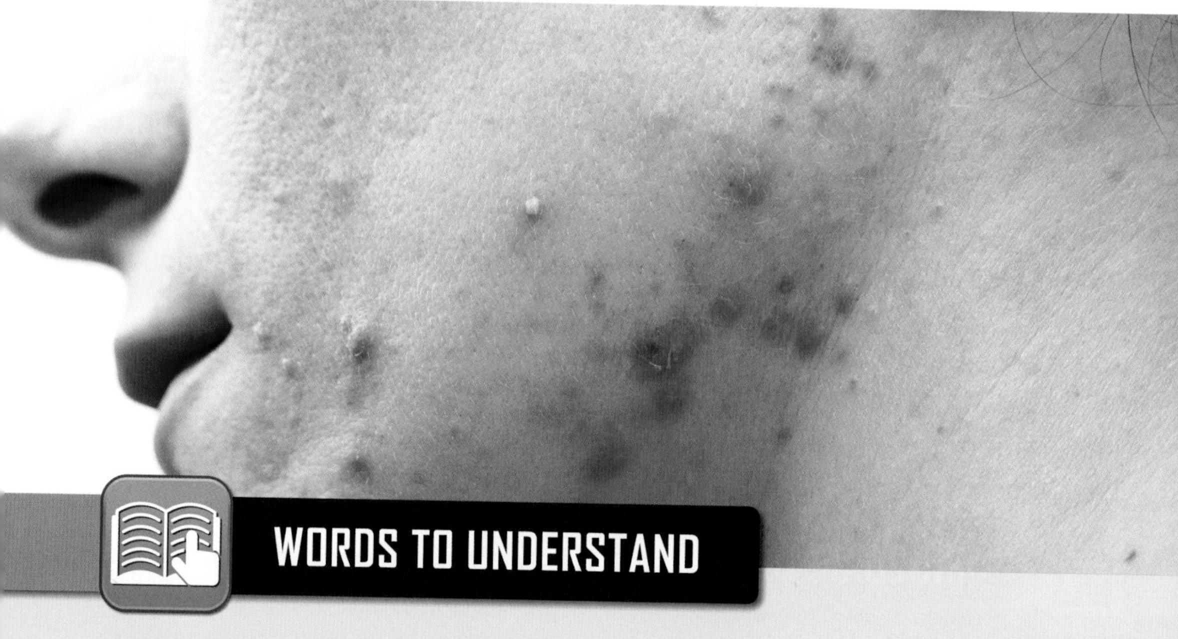

### WORDS TO UNDERSTAND

**adolescence:** the teen years.

**erythema:** a general term that is used for the redness and swelling of the skin.

**birthmark:** a permanent mark on the skin, usually brown or red.

## Port Wine Stain

A port wine stain is a unique type of birthmark that appears on the skin. Initially, the stain is pink in color but with increasing time it becomes red to purple. The color develops due to the swelling of the underlying blood vessels. The stain usually occurs on the face and can be removed surgically and by laser therapies.

## Dandruff

Dandruff is another type of skin problem that affects the scalp. A thin layer of dead skin cells that are pushed off the scalp form the dandruff. A certain amount of dandruff is normal but an increased amount of dandruff can cause discomfort and lead to skin allergies. Regular use of anti-dandruff shampoo can help reduce the dandruff.

## Sunburn

A sunburn refers to burning of the skin due to overexposure to the sun, such as while swimming or on the beach. The sun's rays are made up of different types of UV rays that are harmful for the skin. As a result of the sunburn the skin turns red.
In severe cases the person may feel dizziness and fatigue.
Sunburns can be treated by use of medicines, but the best course is to prevent them entirely by using sunscreen.

## Erythema

Erythema of the skin can arise due to any injury, underlying skin disease, acne medication, allergies, waxing and tweezing of the hairs. Erythema can occur on any part of the skin. A doctor should be consulted for proper treatment.

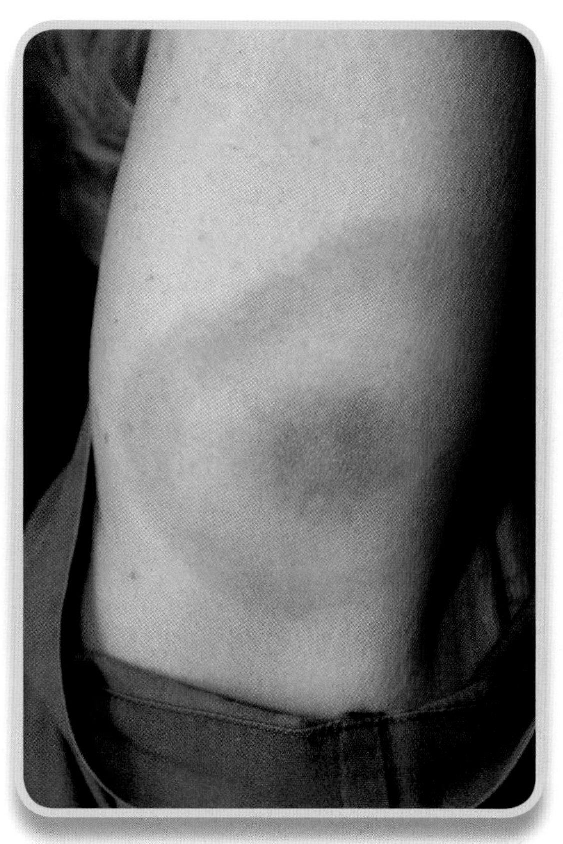

## Cancer

Cancers are an unrestrained growth of cells. There are a number of different types of skin cancer, some more serious than others. They include basal cell cancer, squamous cell skin carcinoma, and the most serious type, melanoma. Skin cancers are usually curable but they need to be addressed as soon as possible.

### SIDEBAR: DID YOU KNOW?

- Squeezing pimples can leave permanent scars on the face.
- Your skin accounts for roughly 15 percent of your body weight.

# IMMUNE SYSTEM DISEASES

The immune system is the defensive system that helps the body to fight off infections. It fights off infection through a series of complex reactions that take place one after the other. The immune system is made up of many different types of cells, tissues, and organs. It is frequently attacked by diseases.

## Diabetes Mellitus

Type 1 diabetes mellitus is an inflammatory autoimmune disease of the pancreas. A person suffering from diabetes is not able to produce enough insulin, a hormone that helps to regulate carbohydrate and fat metabolism. This form of diabetes is generally controlled by administering insulin.

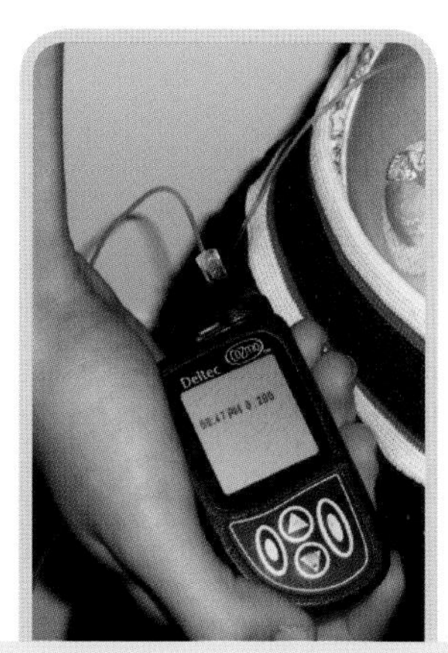

## WORDS TO UNDERSTAND

**antigen:** a foreign substance that causes an immune reaction.

**autoimmune:** a type of illness in which the body's immune system mistakenly attacks the body.

**immunodeficiency:** describes a failure of the immune system.

**pancreas:** an organ that produces hormones called insulin and glucagon.

## Primary Immunodeficiency

Primary immunodeficiency disorders occur when a part of the immune system is either missing from the body or does not function properly. Such disorders may occur due to excessive use of medicines and drugs, other diseases, and exposure to chemicals. These diseases weaken the immune system and make it prone to other type of infections.

## Graves's Disease

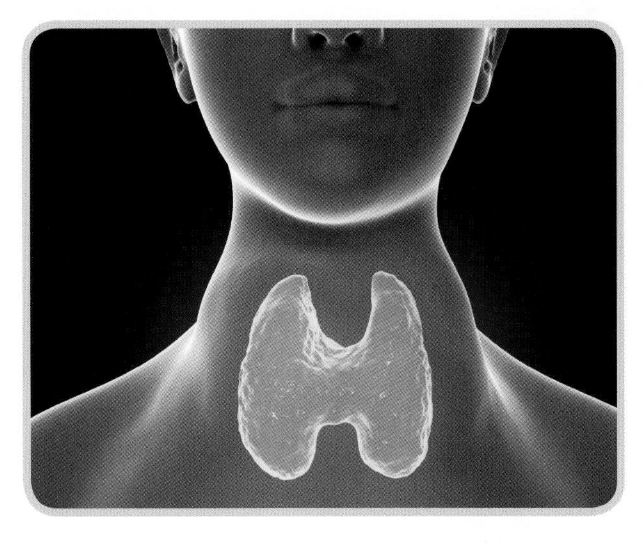

Graves's disease is a type of autoimmune disorder. An excess release of the thyroid hormone from the thyroid gland leads to the Graves's disease. A higher production of thyroid hormone causes eye and vision problems, heat intolerance, goiter, insomnia, and increased appetite. The disease can be controlled by the use of medicines and surgery.

## Scleroderma

Scleroderma is an autoimmune disorder that leads to deposits of collagen protein under the skin. The affected person experiences thickening and hardening of the skin of the hands, face, stiffness of the body, and joint pain. Scleroderma cannot be cured but the symptoms can be reduced with medication.

## Rheumatic Fever

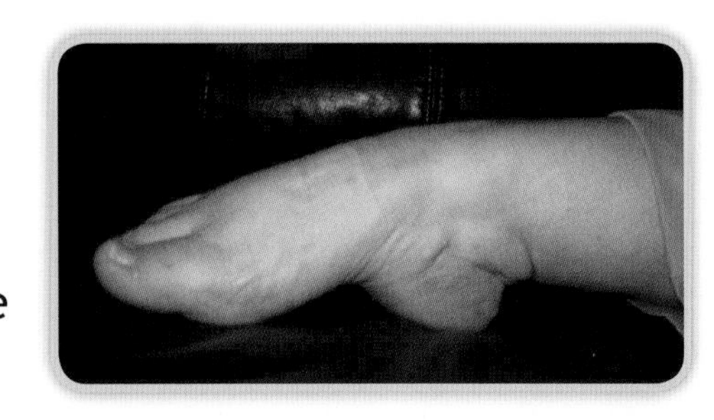

Rheumatic fever is an autoimmune inflammatory disease. It is caused by bacteria and causes the swelling of the heart valves, brain, skin, and joints.

The disease commonly affects children who are between 6 and 15 years of age. It can result from inadequately treated strep throat. The disease is characterized by the presence of fever, abdominal pain, heart problems, skin problems, and muscle weakness. The disease is very serious but can be treated with the use of antibiotics.

## Pernicious Anemia

Pernicious anemia is an autoimmune disorder that occurs in an individual when there is extremely low absorption of vitamin B12 from the digestive tract. Vitamin B12 helps in proper development and functioning of the red blood cells. Due to the lack of this vitamin, very low levels of red blood cells are found in the blood. This may lead to lack of energy, loss of appetite, pale-colored skin, swollen and bleeding tongue, or numbness of the hands and feet. Eating a balanced diet and taking vitamin B12 supplements can help manage the disease.

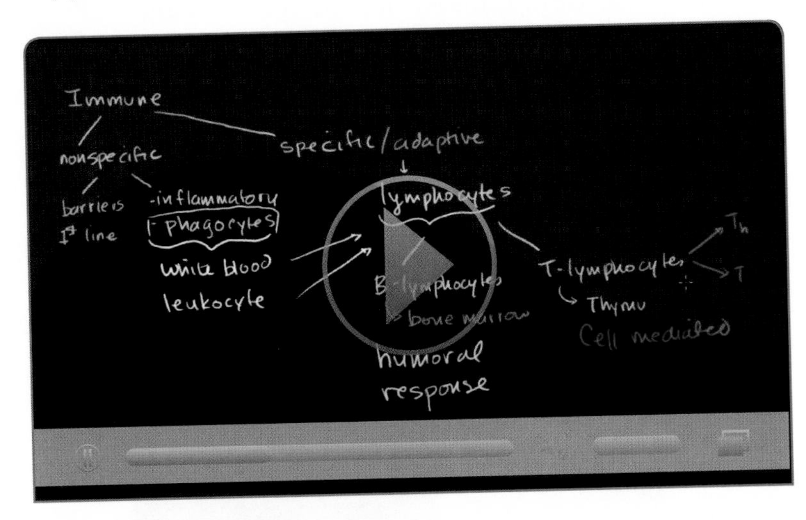


This video explains the various types of immune responses.

### SIDEBAR: DID YOU KNOW?

- Whenever your body is exposed to a new antigen, it creates new antibodies to fight it.
- The immune disorder known as Graves's disease was named after the Irish physician who discovered it, Robert Graves.

# HORMONAL IMBALANCES

Hormones regulate the functions of different body parts and help in the overall growth of the body. A hormonal imbalance occurs when a hormone is released in amounts that are either too low or too high. These hormonal imbalances cause different types of diseases and disorders in the human body. Some common symptoms of hormonal imbalance are fatigue, mood swings, and weight problems.

## Gigantism and Dwarfism

Gigantism and dwarfism are the most common disorders caused due to the varying levels of the growth hormone. An excessive level of the growth hormone leads to gigantism while an extremely low level leads to dwarfism. Individuals suffering from gigantism are very tall and have abnormally large body parts while people with dwarfism have an extremely short stature. People with gigantism and dwarfism can be at risk for certain other types of diseases.

## WORDS TO UNDERSTAND

**fatigue:** a condition of extreme tiredness.

**hormone:** a chemical substance that is released in the bloodstream.

**puberty:** the period in which young people reach sexual maturity and become capable of reproduction.

**thyroid:** gland that regulate the rate of growth and metabolism.

## Precocious Puberty

Precocious puberty is not a disease or disorder but is a condition causing the early onset of puberty. Individuals experiencing precocious puberty mature earlier than other individuals of the same age group. Different hormones are produced in the bodies of girls and boys during puberty. These hormones lead to the development and maturation of sexual characteristics in an individual. Several factors such as genetic structure, dietary changes, hormonal activities, and body structure play a role in deciding the time of onset of puberty.

## Goiter

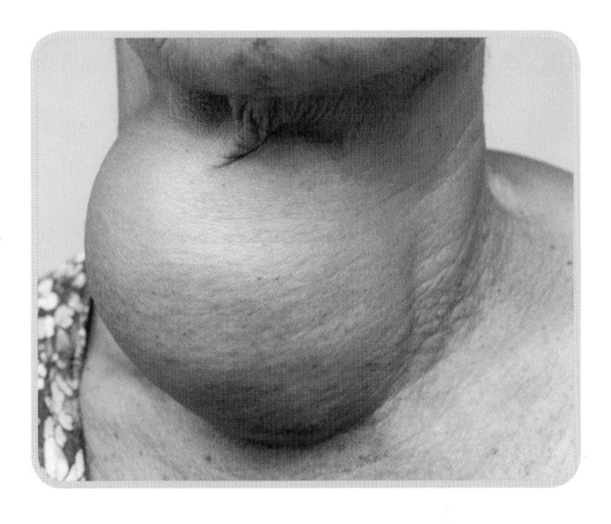

Goiter is the disease caused by the enlargement of the thyroid gland, leading to a visible lump and swelling in the front part of the neck. A person suffering from goiter may produce normal, excess, or lower levels of the thyroid hormone. The condition is usually painless and may be accompanied by frequent coughing, difficulties in swallowing, breathing problems, and voice changes. Proper medication and treatment is available for the disease and people can completely get rid of the problem.

## Acromegaly

Acromegaly is a growth disorder that is caused due to excess production of growth hormone in an adult. The condition causes abrupt growth and swelling of certain tissues due to accumulation of growth hormone in the tissues. The disease leads to reduced muscle strength, enlarged bones and muscles, excessive perspiration, widened teeth. The disease can be cured by the use of medication, radiation therapy, or surgery to remove the part of the brain that produces the extra hormone.

# Osteoporosis

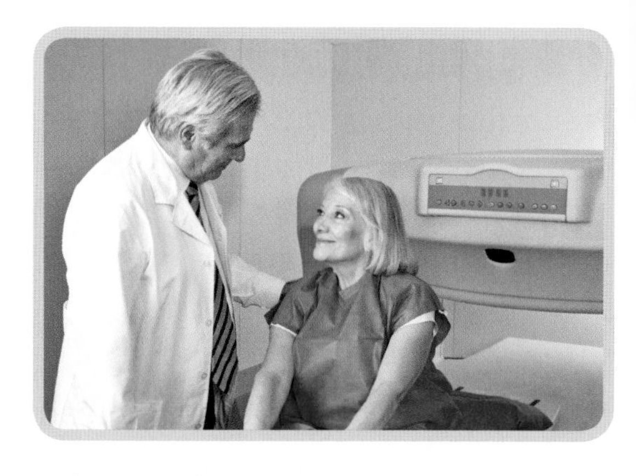

Osteoporosis is a disease of the bones caused by the release of certain hormones of the parathyroid gland. The condition leads to frequent bone fractures, pain in the bones and joints, and neck and back pains. The condition is most common in older women. The use of specific medicines, hormone injections, and dietary changes can help treat the disease at an early stage.

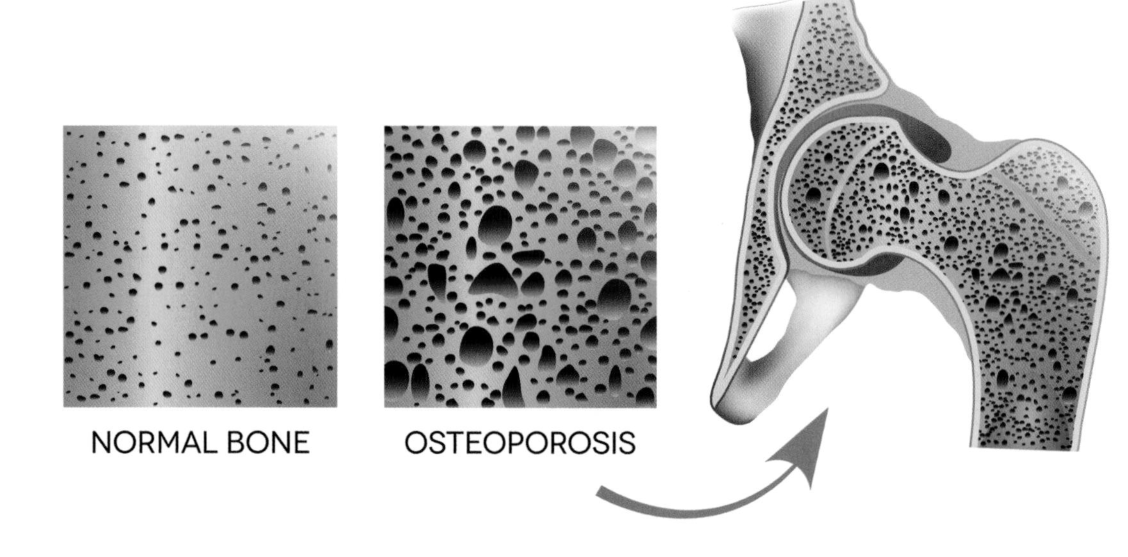

## SIDEBAR: DID YOU KNOW?

- Osteoporosis is more common in women than in men.
- There are around 30,000 Americans with dwarfism.

# ALLERGIES

Allergies are a type of response of the immune system to any foreign particle that is not otherwise harmful. Allergies are also known as a hypersensitivity of the body. Types of allergens known to cause allergy in human beings are pollen, dust, sunlight, temperature changes, pet dander, molds, certain fragrances, cosmetics, flowers, and certain food items. The allergens may lead to or aggravate certain types of illnesses and diseases in human beings.

## Histamine

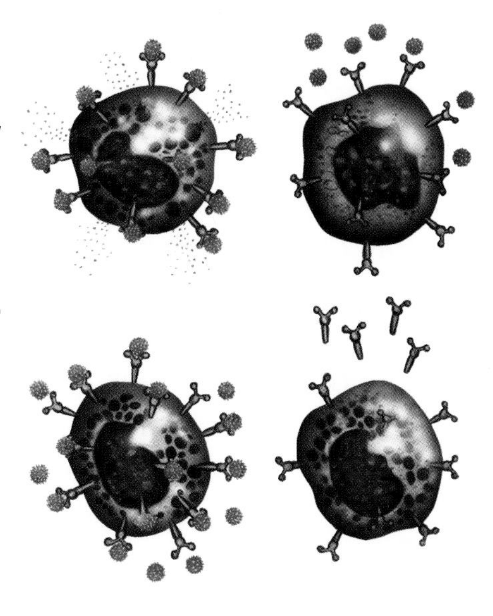

An allergen can enter the body through any of the sense organs—eyes, ears, skin, mouth, and nose. Whenever an allergen enters the body, the immune system produces a response. The immune response refers to the production of a set of reactions and chemicals that are secreted to fight off the infections. These chemicals are known as histamines and are made up of proteins. The histamines are directly released into the blood vessels, which causes the swelling, itching, and redness of the area where the allergen is present.

## WORDS TO UNDERSTAND

allergens: substances that cause allergic reactions in the body.
atopic dermatitis: a condition involving red, itchy skin.
dander: tiny particles, such as dead skin, that are shed by animals.
seasonal: describes something that occurs at regular times of year.

## Eye Allergies

Allergens like dust, pollen, dandruff, and cosmetics can lead to itching, watering, and redness of the eyes. Eye allergies can also lead to problems such as nasal allergies, sinus, and pink eye. Maintaining proper cleanliness, avoiding places of dust and debris, frequently washing the eyes and using eye drops can help in reducing the occurrence of eye allergies.

## Hay Fever

Hay fever, or allergic rhinitis, is a seasonal allergy of the eyes and nose that frequently occurs during the spring. Hay fever is characterized by the presence of red, swollen, watery eyes, sneezing and blocked nose. The basic treatment available for hay fever includes the use of anti-allergic medicines and corticosteroids. However, the basic preventive measure is to avoid places of high dust and pollen concentration.

## Food Allergies

Food allergy occurs when the immune system generates an immune response for a particular food item. Individuals can be allergic to peanuts, shellfish, milk, soy, eggs, wheat, and many other things. Food allergy must be carefully diagnosed with the help of a doctor.

## Animal Allergies

Animal allergies are allergic reactions that are caused or aggravated by animal fur, urine, saliva, or dung. Allergic reactions may include hay fever, asthma, rashes, and atopic dermatitis.

Close proximity to pets such as cats, dogs, rats, hamsters, and horses will bring out a reaction in people who are allergic.

## Photosensitivity

Sensitivity or allergy to sunlight (or strong light from another source) is known as photosensitivity. Photosensitivity affects the skin of the affected individual and may lead to several other skin problems. People with photosensitivity are more prone to be affected by sunburns and skin cancer. Use of sunscreens, antibiotics, and other medicines may help reduce photosensitivity. In addition, care should be taken to avoid traveling in strong sunlight.

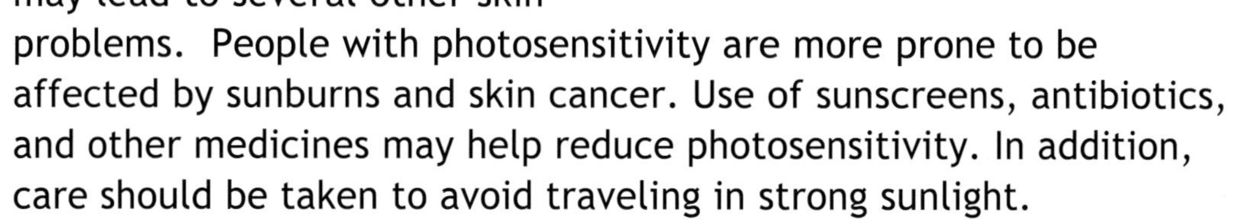

## Plant Allergies

Plants or plant products can also serve as allergens. Several raw fruits and vegetables, flowers, peanuts, poison ivy, poison oak, and poison sumac can lead to eye, nasal, and skin allergies. The plant products may instantly cause an allergy or may take several days for the symptoms to show up. The symptoms include the formation of colored patches, red rashes, and blisters on the skin.

### SIDEBAR: DID YOU KNOW?

- **About 50 million Americans have at least one allergy.**
- **Allergies have no cures. They can only be managed by avoiding the allergen or receiving prompt treatment after exposure.**

# MUSCULOSKELETAL DISORDERS

Bones, muscles, and joints are a part of the musculoskeletal system. The skeletal system forms the supporting framework for the body and gives a fixed shape and form to the body. The maximum weight of a human being's body is made up of the bones and muscles. The bones, muscles, and joints of the body are also susceptible to several diseases, breakage and disorders.

## Bone Fracture

A bone fracture is an injury to a bone that causes cracking or breakage. A fracture can occur in the bones of any body part such as an arm, leg, hip, backbone, ribs, and so on. A bone fracture is a very common condition that affects the people of all age groups. It can occur for several reasons such as bone diseases, a fall from a height, and or accidents. Different types of fractures are treated in different ways. Usually a cast is applied to keep the injured bone in place and help with healing.

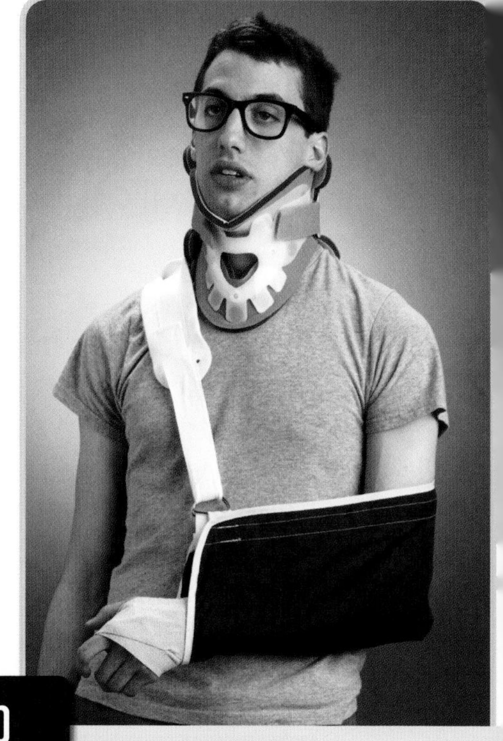

## WORDS TO UNDERSTAND

cartilage: a type of flexible connective tissue that provides cushioning to joints.
joints: here, the points at which two bones are connected.
physical therapy: the treatment of injury or disease with techniques such as massage and exercise instead of (or in addition to) surgery or medication.

## Sports Injuries

Sports injuries are a common type of injury that occurs while exercising or playing games. These injuries may affect any part of the bone, muscle, or joints. Several types of injuries that may occur are sprains and strains, knee injuries, muscle pains, bone fractures, and bone dislocations. Treatment includes proper rest, use of pain relievers, and surgery.

## Clubfoot

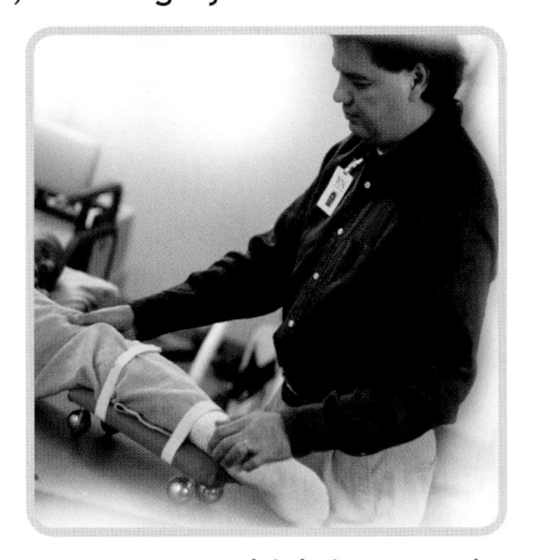

Clubfoot is a birth defect of the muscle and bone tissue of the feet. This condition causes the foot to be turned inwards and downwards. The muscles of the affected foot are shorter than normal, but the cause of this abnormality is not known. The foot may be flexible or rigid and has reduced movement. Foot reshaping treatment is generally used for this problem. It is a long treatment which is started soon after birth and is carried out by a bone specialist.

## Gout

Gout is a form of arthritis that affects the joints of the body. The problem occurs due to excess amount of uric acid deposits in the blood. People suffering from diabetes, kidney diseases, obesity, and blood cancers are at a higher risk of developing gout. The problem usually begins from the toe, knee, or ankle joints in the feet and leads to

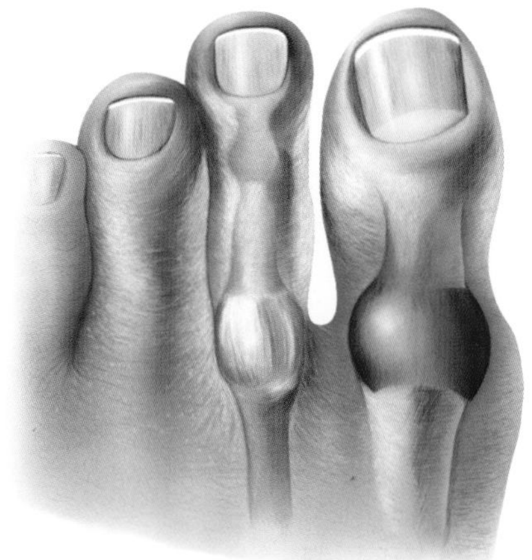

painful, swollen, and stiff joints. The incidences of the disease can be reduced with the help of pain reducing medicines, anti-inflammatory drugs, and a few dietary changes and avoiding the consumption of alcohol.

## Osteoarthritis

Osteoarthritis is a type of degenerative disease of the joint. The main cause of the disease is the destruction of cartilage. Cartilage is present between two bones around the joints and helps in smooth movement of the bones. The destruction of the cartilage causes friction in the bones when they move against each other. This condition leads to the wear and tear of joints, causing persistent pain, swelling, and stiffness. The disease is incurable but the symptoms can be controlled by repeated surgeries and medication.

## Rheumatoid Arthritis

Rheumatoid arthritis is an autoimmune disease of the joints. The immune system of the body itself attacks the healthy joints and leads to their inflammation. The disease commonly affects the wrists, fingers, knees, feet, and ankle joints. The joints become tender, develop pain, and become deformed with time. It involves lifelong treatment including physical therapy, exercise, medicines, and surgery.

## SIDEBAR: DID YOU KNOW?

- **Clubfoot is usually a painless condition.**
- **Warming up the body by doing light stretching exercises before playing sports helps in reducing injuries.**

# URINARY SYSTEM DISORDERS

The urinary system works continuously to filter the blood and extract waste products from it. These waste products are further filtered and the important nutrients and water is absorbed back. The liquid waste called urine is ejected from the body. The urinary system is also affected by several diseases and disorders, some minor and some serious.

## Urinary Tract Infection

A urinary tract infection (UTI) can occur in any part of the urinary system. The most common type of UTI is urethritis, which affects the urethra, a tube that empties the urine from the bladder. UTIs are more common in women than men.

A person suffering from UTI will likely experience pain or burning sensation during urination. Other symptoms include fever, cloudy urine, foul-smelling urine, fatigue and fever, and lower abdominal pain. UTIs are unpleasant but highly treatable. Different types of medicines are used to cure urinary tract infections.

### WORDS TO UNDERSTAND

dehydration: a state of having insufficient water in the body.
dialysis: the separation of particles in a liquid.
tract: a major passage of the body, such as the digestive tract or urinary tract.

## Kidney Stones

Kidney stones are another common problem of the urinary system. The "stones" are actually crystalline deposits in the kidneys. One cause is prolonged dehydration; the lack of water causes urine to become more concentrated. Obesity can also contribute to kidney stones, as can certain types of diets, such as a high-protein diet. Kidney stones cause severe pain, swelling of the kidneys, and UTIs. In most of the cases, the stones move out of the body through the urinary tract on their own, but in some cases surgical removal is required.

## Hematuria

Hematuria is a medical condition in which a large number of red blood cells are passed in the urine. The condition can often be recognized due to the red color of the urine. Hematuria may occur due to extremely high levels of stress or trauma. It can also be brought on by UTIs, kidney stones, and some types of cancers. Anyone finding blood in their urine should consult with a doctor immediately—hematuria is often a very minor problem but it's sometimes a sign of something more serious.

## Kidney Failure

Kidney failure is a serious condition in which the kidneys do not function properly and the amount of wastes in the body increases. It may affect either one or both of the kidneys. It may lead to several other problems such as poisoning of the body, an increase in blood pressure, anemia, delayed healing from injury and the inhibition of body functions. In the case of kidney failures, kidney transplants and dialysis can be carried out.

A dialysis machine is a large instrument which is used to perform the function of the kidney. How often dialysis is needed depends on the stage of kidney failure; some patients may require dialysis twice a month, while some may require dialysis in every three days. In this procedure the impure blood from the vein in the patient's hand enters the dialyzer and the purified blood is returned through the artery in the same hand. Dialysis is a useful process, keeps a good check on body processes, and requires less dietary changes. However, it is a complex and time-consuming process.

## SIDEBAR: DID YOU KNOW?

- **Drinking a lot of water can help small-sized kidney stones to flush naturally out of body.**
- **A physical blow to the kidneys can result in hematuria.**

# HIV/AIDS

Acquired Immunodeficiency Syndrome (AIDS) is a viral disease of the immune system. The disease is caused by the HIV virus which weakens the immune system over time. This makes infected individuals susceptible to other diseases. AIDS is the final stage of HIV infection. AIDS was first reported in the United States during the 1980s. To date around 30 million people worldwide have died from the disease.

## HIV

Human immunodeficiency virus (HIV) is a unique and potentially deadly virus. It is called a retrovirus because it multiplies in the host cell by mixing with the host cell's DNA. It can easily move from one cell to the other to spread infection. Most HIV-positive people develop the disease AIDS sooner or later. Only a few people who are infected with HIV do not develop the disease; they are known as long-term nonprogressors.

### WORDS TO UNDERSTAND

**antiretroviral:** describes a type of treatment that is effective against retroviruses like HIV.

**HIV-positive:** describes someone who carries the HIV virus.

**opportunistic:** describes something that exploits an opening or opportunity.

## Stages

Different stages are involved in the development of AIDS from the HIV infection.These are the window period, the latent period, the symptomatic period and AIDS.

- The window period marks the beginning of the HIV infection and exists for a period of a few weeks to a few months.
- The latent period is the asymptomatic period during which no symptoms are shown. It may continue for a time span of a few months to several years.
- The symptomatic period is the period of increased virus activity. In this period, different infections occur repeatedly and weaken the body.
- AIDS is the final stage of the viral infection. During this period, the body is characterized with several opportunistic infections.

## Symptoms

The symptoms of the disease do not appear immediately after the infection. There is always a lag between the infection and the appearance of the symptoms. Symptoms arise due to different types of opportunistic infections. Opportunistic infections attack people with weak immune system but are harmless to people with strong immune systems. People affected with AIDS commonly suffer from night chills and sweats, swollen lymph glands, weakness, and abrupt weight loss.

## Modes of Transmission

The transmission of the virus from one person to another can happen in a few specific ways. The HIV virus is easily spread through the blood transfusion processes, but blood banks routinely screen blood for HIV, so this is now an unlikely transmission method.  However, intravenous drug users who share needles are at high risk of HIV because small amounts of blood are passed by way of the needle. The other significant method of HIV transmission is through sexual intercourse. Expectant mothers who are HIV-positive are at risk of sharing the virus with their unborn children—however, if the mother's virus is being treated, that risk becomes very low. HIV virus does not spread through touching, sitting with, or hugging an infected person.

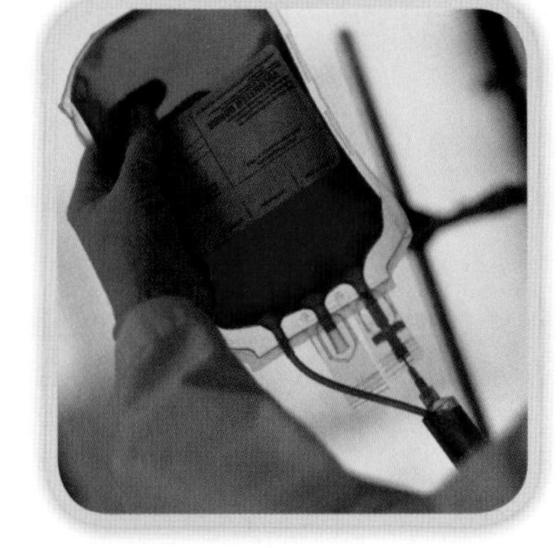

## Treatment

At present, there is no cure for the disease. However, HIV/AIDS is no longer a "death sentence" the way it once was. Treatment is complex and expensive, but many patients are able to manage their conditions. Numerous medications and treatments are available to delay the onset of disease, control the symptoms, and cure the opportunistic infections. One such effective treatment is antiretroviral therapy (ART). ART has the additional benefit of making it less likely for people to transmit the virus to others.

### SIDEBAR: DID YOU KNOW?

- **According to a report, 34 million people were struck by AIDS as of 2010.**
- **Research indicates that HIV originated in the western part of Central Africa during the early 20th century**

# CANCERS AND TUMORS

A tumor is an abnormal condition in which the cells of a particular part of the body keep on growing and dividing. The tumors may or may not be visible externally. Tumors are usually of two types—benign and malignant. Benign tumors are restricted to one part of the body and don't spread. Malignant tumors are also called "cancerous" tumors and they can spread to other parts the body.

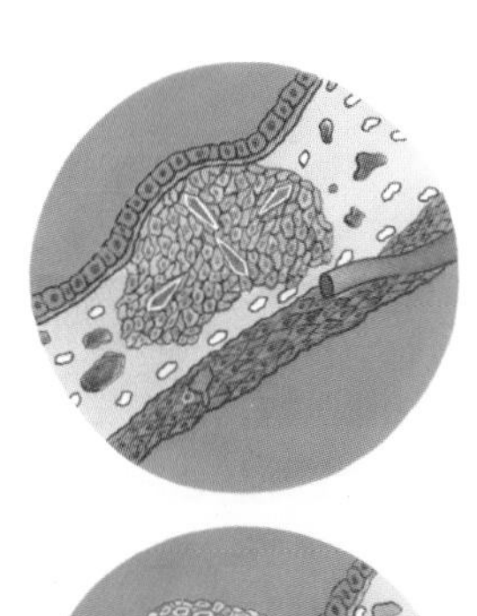

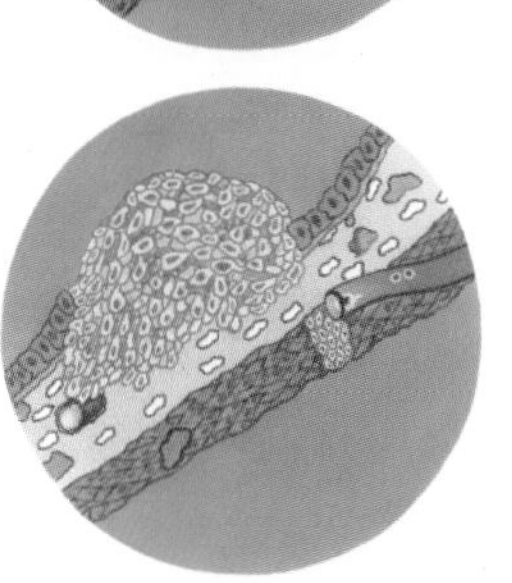

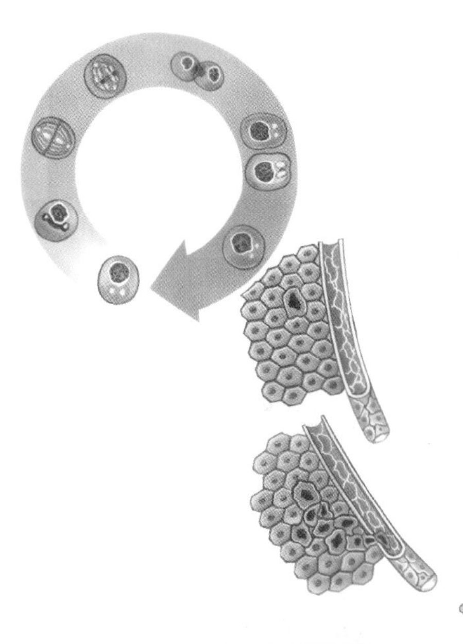

## Lung Cancer

Lung cancer is a common type of cancer of the respiratory system. It may affect any part including the air tubes and lungs. Smoking cigarettes is the leading cause of

### WORDS TO UNDERSTAND

**benign:** not harmful.
**chemotherapy:** treatment of cancers using specific chemicals that kill cells.
**malignant:** very harmful.

lung cancer, but it can also be caused by exposure to certain pollutants. Common symptoms include bloody coughs, chest pain, recurring pneumonia, loss of appetite, and fatigue. Lung cancer may be curable if it's caught early.

## Brain Tumors

Brain tumors can affect any part of the brain such as brain cells, nerves, or supporting glands. When a brain tumor begins in the brain, it's called a primary brain tumor; when it's the result of tumors elsewhere that have spread to the brain, it's called a secondary brain tumor. The exact reasons for the occurrence of brain tumor are unknown, although family history seems to play a role, as does exposure to radiation. Brain tumors produce some very easily recognizable symptoms. These include severe headaches, seizures, changes in mental ability, changes in taste, smell, hearing, and a sudden inability to read or write. If diagnosed at the right time, brain tumors can be cured by surgery, radiation therapy, and chemotherapy.

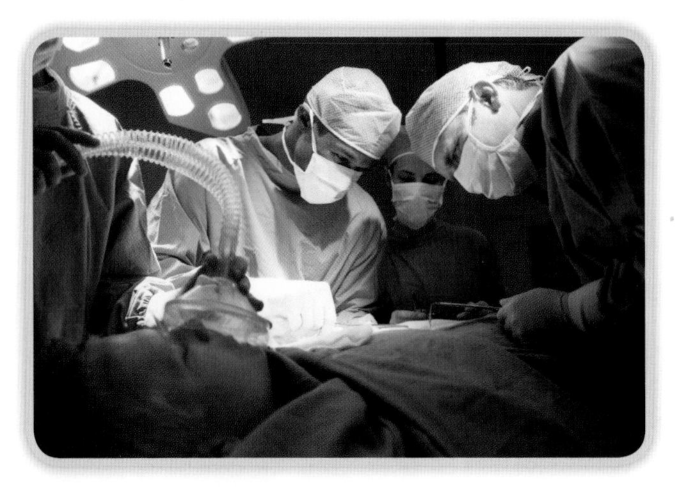

## Leukemia

Leukemia is a type of blood cancer. This condition produces abnormal white blood cells in the bone marrow. A person suffering from leukemia is prone to several types of infections, anemia, and weight loss due to weak white blood cells. Leukemia cannot be prevented but survival rates are improving steadily every year due to improved therapies.

## Skin Cancer

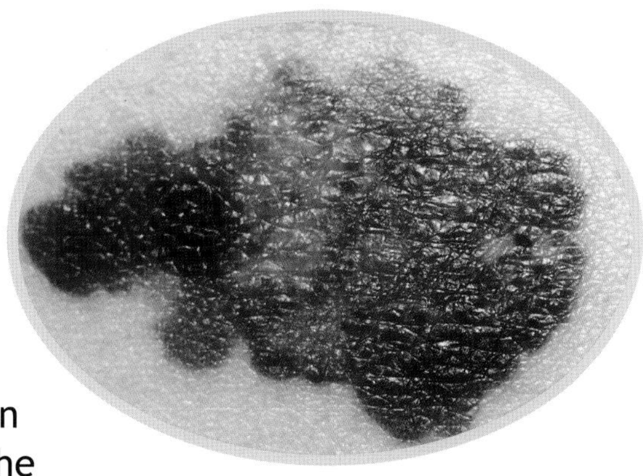
Melanoma

Skin cancer is the type of cancer which affects the skin cells. Skin Cancer usually appears on the head, neck, face, and arms. The most common causes of skin cancer are repeated or prolonged sunburns and a family history of skin cancer. The skin cancer begins at the cells of the outermost skin layer, the epidermis. A different type of skin cancer that begins in the melanocytes (cells that give skin its color) is melanoma. The emergence of the cancer usually occurs as a nonhealing sore on the skin.

## Oral Cancer

The cancerous condition of the mouth is known as oral cancer. It may occur in any part of the mouth such as the lips, tongue, cheeks, floor of the mouth, gums, and palate. Oral cancers occur mostly as a result of smoking or chewing tobacco, poor oral hygiene, and repeated oral problems. The cancer usually begins as a dark-colored mouth ulcer or as white plaque, and gradually spreads in the whole mouth. The condition is usually painless at first but may become very painful later, causing difficulties in speech as well as swallowing food. Like other forms of cancer, it is curable if diagnosed early.

### SIDEBAR: DID YOU KNOW?

- There are more than 200 types of cancers.
- Leukemia is the most common cancer in children and teenagers; even so, it is still quite rare.

# GENETIC DISORDERS

A gene is the smallest, basic functional unit of **heredity**. Our genes come from our parents, which is why physical characteristics, height, and other features of children are similar to their parents. Diseases likewise can "run in the family." Certain families are more prone to having high cholesterol, for example, while others aren't. There is also a class of diseases specifically called "genetic disorders," which occur when part of a gene is missing or faulty. Some genetic diseases can be life threatening, but many are manageable.

## WORDS TO UNDERSTAND

**coagulation:** here, blood clotting.
**heredity:** the passing of traits from parents to children.
**stem cell:** a cell that has not yet become a particular type of cell ("undifferentiated"), so it is able to be turned into a variety of different cells for medical use.

## Muscular Dystrophy

Muscular dystrophy (MD) is a genetic disorder that affects the muscles. Due to missing or damaged genes, affected individuals are not able to produce particular proteins that keep the muscles healthy. MD is a degenerative disease that can complicate even simple activities like standing or walking. The disease can affect the muscles of any part of the body. MD is more common in boys than girls. There is no cure for MD, but treatments that slow the progression of the disease exist.

## Hemophilia

Hemophilia is a blood-related genetic disorder in which the blood does not clot normally. The disease is caused by a faulty part of a gene that doesn't produce a particular protein known as a coagulation factor. Although the disease is rare, it can prove to be fatal if excessive blood loss occurs or if the blood loss occurs in the brain. Hemophilia can range from mild to severe. Treatment involves the injection of blood clotting factor. Hemophilia used to be called "the royal disease" because an unusual number European royals suffered from it.

## Sickle Cell Anemia

Sickle cell is a condition that affects the blood, causing blood cells become crescent shaped. Such types of cells are unable to transport enough oxygen to the body. They also can clog the blood vessels, obstructing blood flow. A person suffering from sickle cell anemia can experience attacks of severe pain, fatigue, frequent infections, strokes, and delayed growth. Sickle cell anemia patients required a great deal of treatment, including blood transfusions and pain killers. Gene therapy may hold the key to a cure for sickle cell. In 2017, a sickle cell patient in Kansas City, Kansas was declared to have been cured, thanks to donated stem cells.

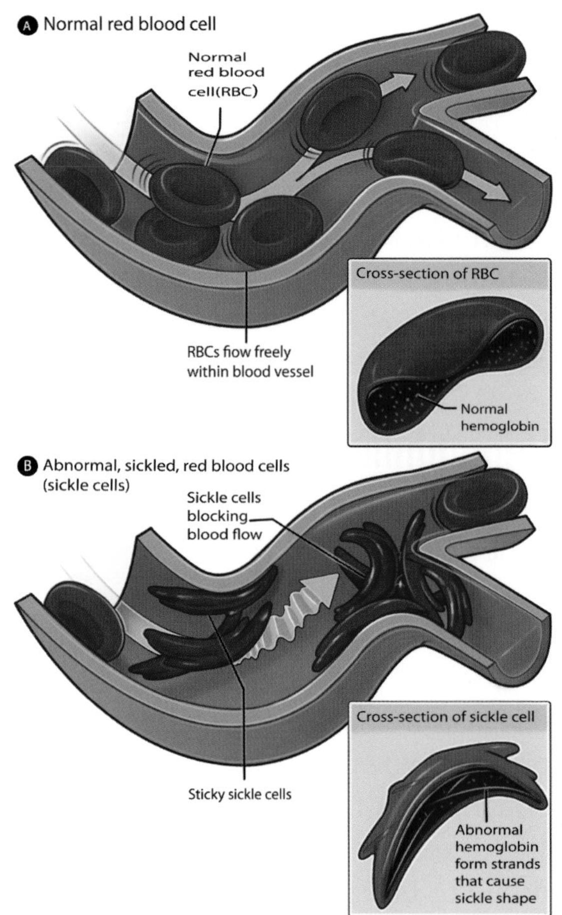


## Thalassemia

Thalassemia is another blood-related genetic disorder. In this disorder, the body does not produce the blood protein hemoglobin. This limits the the oxygen-carrying ability of the blood. Affected people suffer from mild to severe anemia, fatigue, bone deformities, growth abnormalities, and jaundice. The disease is managed using medicines and blood transfusions.

## Albinism

Albinism is a type of genetic disorder characterized by a lack of the skin pigment called melanin. Affected

individuals have light-colored eyes, skin, and hair. The missing pigment also causes several vision- and skin-related problems, such as poor eyesight or even blindness, easily damaged skin, and the risk of developing skin cancers. Individuals with albinism have to avoid strong sunlight, use sunscreens and sunglasses while in the sun, and may even need to undergo eye surgery.

A personal story about muscular dystrophy.

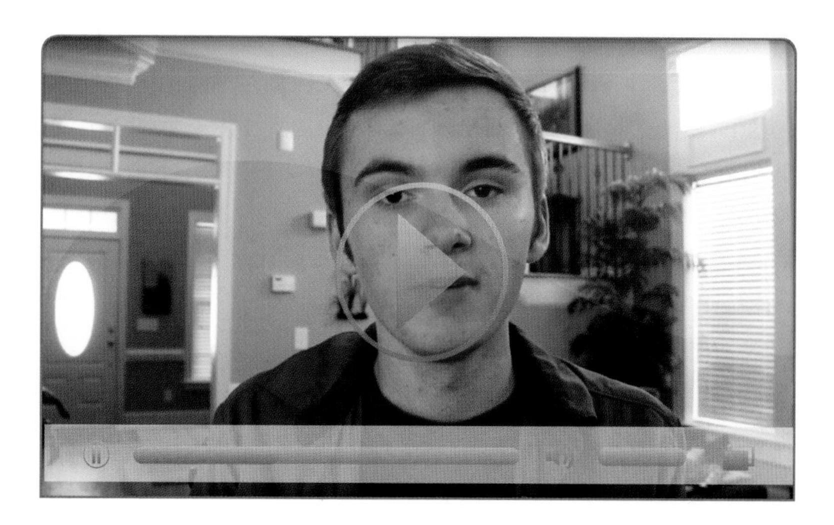

## SIDEBAR: DID YOU KNOW?

- Historians believe that hemophilia might have played a role in sparking the Russian Revolution. The children of Tsar Nicholas II suffered from the condition and their mother turned to an advisor named Grigori Rasputin for help. The much-hated Rasputin's close relationship with the royal family probably hastened their execution in 1918.
- According to the March of Dimes organization, every year 7.8 million children in the world are born with a serious genetic disorder.

# OCCUPATIONAL HEALTH HAZARDS

Occupational diseases refer to any illness that a person might acquire due to his involvement with a particular industry. People are exposed to various biological, chemical, and physical factors present at workplaces. The impact may be instant, while others may take years to surface. Most occupational diseases are preventable with regular evaluation of the work environment and strict enforcement of safety regulations.

## In History

Occupational diseases are not strictly a modern problem. One of the earliest references to occupational disease dates back to Hippocrates's third book of *Epidemics* written in 400 BC where he mentions metal extraction workers suffering from stomach problems. With the dawn of the industrial revolution in the 17th century, occupational diseases grew tremendously. Most industries during this period functioned in unhygienic conditions.

## WORDS TO UNDERSTAND

**acclimatization:** the process of gradually getting used to a new condition or climate.

**carcinogens:** cancer-causing agents.

**fire-retardant:** a substance that can stop or slow the spread of fire.

Mining became one of the leading causes of diseases among industrial workers. Miners suffered from breathing problems and severe lung disorders. The number of accidents and deaths while at work or due to poor working conditions rose drastically during this period.

## Bernardino Ramazzini

In 1682, a young Italian physician Bernardino Ramazzini became interested in the health problems of workers. He realized many diseases suffered by workers were caused by various work-related factors and working environments. He devised and taught medical courses dedicated to the diseases of workers at the University of Modena. In 1700, he published his knowledge of occupational diseases in *Diseases of Workers*. Ramazzini's contribution to understanding occupational diseases made him known as "the father of occupational medicine."

## Noise

There are many workers around the world who are exposed to extremely high decibels of hazardous sound. People in manufacturing, transportation, agriculture, and mining are at the highest risks. Soldiers are also exposed to loud noise. Constant and regular exposure to loud noise can cause temporary or permanent hearing loss. People working noisy conditions should be equipped with effective ear protection.

## Extreme Temperatures

People in extremely high temperatures may suffer from heat exhaustion resulting in muscle cramps, fatigue, and loss of consciousness, or heat stroke. Meanwhile, people working in extremely cold conditions may suffer from frostbite and hypothermia. Both heat stroke and hypothermia can lead to organ failure resulting in death. Body **acclimatization** and protective clothing can help people working in extreme temperatures.

## Radiation

Exposure to radiation is one of the worst threats faced by many people working in various industries. Radiation has many industrial, medical, and scientific applications. There are two kinds of radiation: ionizing and non-ionizing radiation. People exposed to ionizing radiation may suffer from gastrointestinal disorders, hair loss, and ulcers. High doses of exposure to ionizing radiation can result in brain damage and death. Exposure to non-ionizing radiation can damage the skin and eyes. Protective clothing and eyewear should be worn when a person is working with any form of radiation.

## Occupational Carcinogens

When people talk about how to avoid cancer, they say things like, "just don't start smoking." But what if you are a waiter or bartender, and your job entails spending large amounts of time around other people who smoke? In that case, cigarette smoke is an occupational carcinogen, meaning that your workplace is exposing you to an increased cancer risk. A building material called asbestos is another common occupational carcinogen. Asbestos used to be put in walls and flooring because of its fire-retardant properties. However, asbestos also causes cancer, and anyone engaged in the construction field must take precautions before working around it.

### SIDEBAR: DID YOU KNOW?

- World Health Organization (WHO) has identified more than 300 substances as occupational carcinogens.
- In 2016, more than 5,000 Americans died as a result of workplace injuries.

# PREVENTION AND VACCINATION

If the immune system is weak or hygiene is poor, diseases are more likely to spread. Disease prevention is necessary in order to avoid large-scale spread of diseases and for the overall social and economic growth of society. Different types of diseases can be prevented by different methods.

## Personal Hygiene

Personal hygiene refers to hygiene measures that are followed by individuals. Personal hygiene measures include practices such as bathing, keeping the ears and nose clean, keeping the nails trimmed, washing clothes regularly, and washing hands before and after eating food or using the bathroom.

## Environmental Hygiene

Environmental hygiene refers to the maintenance of clean and healthy living conditions in and around human habitats. Certain practices such as trash removal and regular cleaning of homes and streets need to be

## WORDS TO UNDERSTAND

**attenuated:** weakened.
**eradication:** permanently ending something, such as a disease.
**sewage:** waste that's carried via sewers.
**stagnant:** not moving.

followed. One important hygiene issue in warm areas is stagnant water. Stagnant water offers an ideal breeding ground for mosquitoes, which carry a wide range of infectious diseases. Cleaning up stagnant water can go a long way to making environments more hygienic.

## Community Health

Community health practices include the measures and services that are provided by the government in order to maintain a good health in the region. Governments can take steps to create awareness about diseases and provide healthcare services, such as free or low-cost vaccinations. In addition, governments must assume responsibility for efficient sewage systems, garbage disposal, and the provision of clean and safe drinking water.

## Alterations in Lifestyle

Basic changes in one's lifestyle can help in maintaining a healthy body and reducing the risk of diseases. Getting more sleep, cutting out junk food in favor of a balanced diet, and increasing physical activity are all ways to improve health and strengthen the immune system.

## Vaccination

Vaccination is a method of protecting the body against diseases. A vaccine is a microorganism that is injected in the body to produce an immune response. The body produces antibodies against it to kill the infection. This type of infection is "remembered" by the cells of the immune system and any future attack by the same microorganisms is prevented.

There are a number of different types of vaccines, and which type is used depends on what is most effective against whatever illness is being prevented.

- **Live-attenuated**. These vaccines contain a tiny, weakened amount of the germ that causes the illness. Although the germ is present in a small amount, it just enough to inspire the body to create an immune response. The upside to live-attenuated vaccines is that they usually create a permanent immunity. The downside is that anyone with a compromised immune system needs to be very cautious about using them. (Your doctor can advise on what is safe for you.) Examples of live-attenuated vaccines include the combined measles-mumps-rubella (MMR) vaccine and the chicken pox vaccine.

- **Inactive.** These vaccines use dead versions of the germ. The downside is that they don't create as long-lasting a reaction. This means you may need to get multiple shots (called "boosters") or to get vaccinated every year. The flu vaccine is an example of an inactive vaccine.

- **Toxoid.** These vaccines don't actually make you immune to the germ itself. Instead, they make you immune to the part of the germ that makes you sick. The tetanus vaccine is an example of a toxoid vaccine.

- **Subunit, recombinant, polysaccharide, and conjugate.** Like toxoid vaccines, these vaccines target specific parts of the germ, rather than the entire thing. They cause a strong immune response and they can be used even by people with weakened immune systems. The HPV vaccine is one example.

## Vaccine Benefits

Scientists from the World Health Organization studied the impact of vaccination on global health. They found that vaccination programs around the world have resulted in the following benefits.

- Disease reduction or even eradication
- Lessening severity of diseases that do occur
- Herd immunity (this refers to the idea that even an unvaccinated minority are protected by vaccines if the majority of people get them)
- Healthcare savings

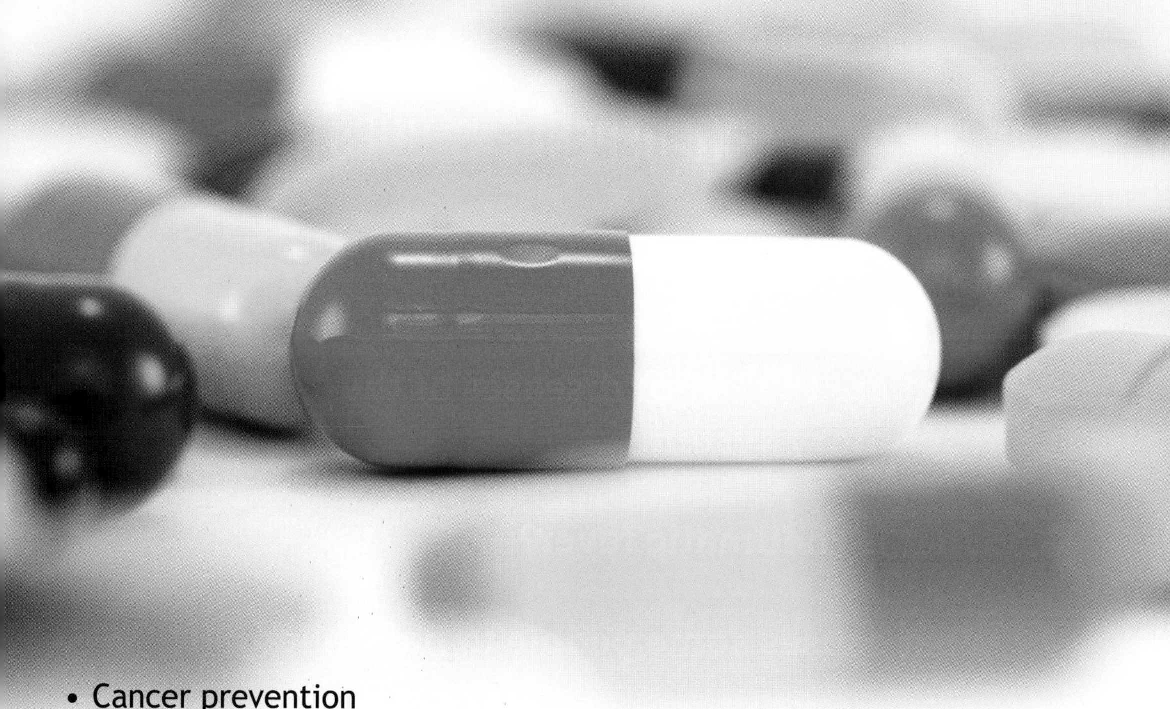

- Cancer prevention
- Lowering chance of antibiotic resistance (because fewer sick people means fewer antibiotics are needed)
- Safer travel
- Empowerment of women (because women are often the caretakers of sick children)
- Economic growth (fewer sick people leads to greater productivity)

## SIDEBAR: DID YOU KNOW?

- It's a myth that you can get the flu from the flu vaccine. Lots of people *feel* like that must have happened to them, but in truth they only received dead flu germs in the vaccine.
- By one estimate, vaccines currently prevent around 6 million deaths per year.

# TEXT-DEPENDENT QUESTIONS

1. What is a vector?
2. What are the major diseases of the respiratory system?
3. What is rheumatic fever?
4. What causes some people to have allergies?
5. What are kidney stones?
6. What causes dwarfism?

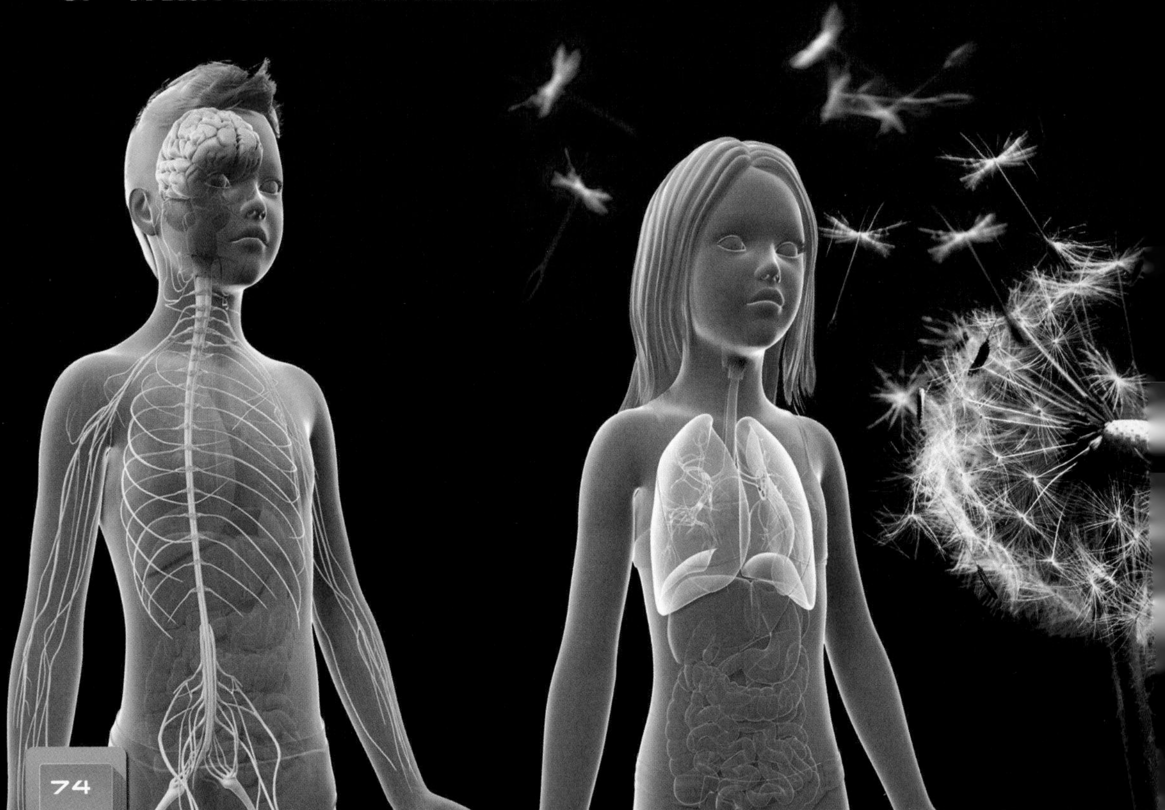

7. Can you catch sickle cell anemia from someone who rides your bus? Why or why not?

8. What role does hygiene play in preventing disease?

9. What is herd immunity?

10. If you get a chicken pox vaccine, will you get chicken pox? Why or why not?

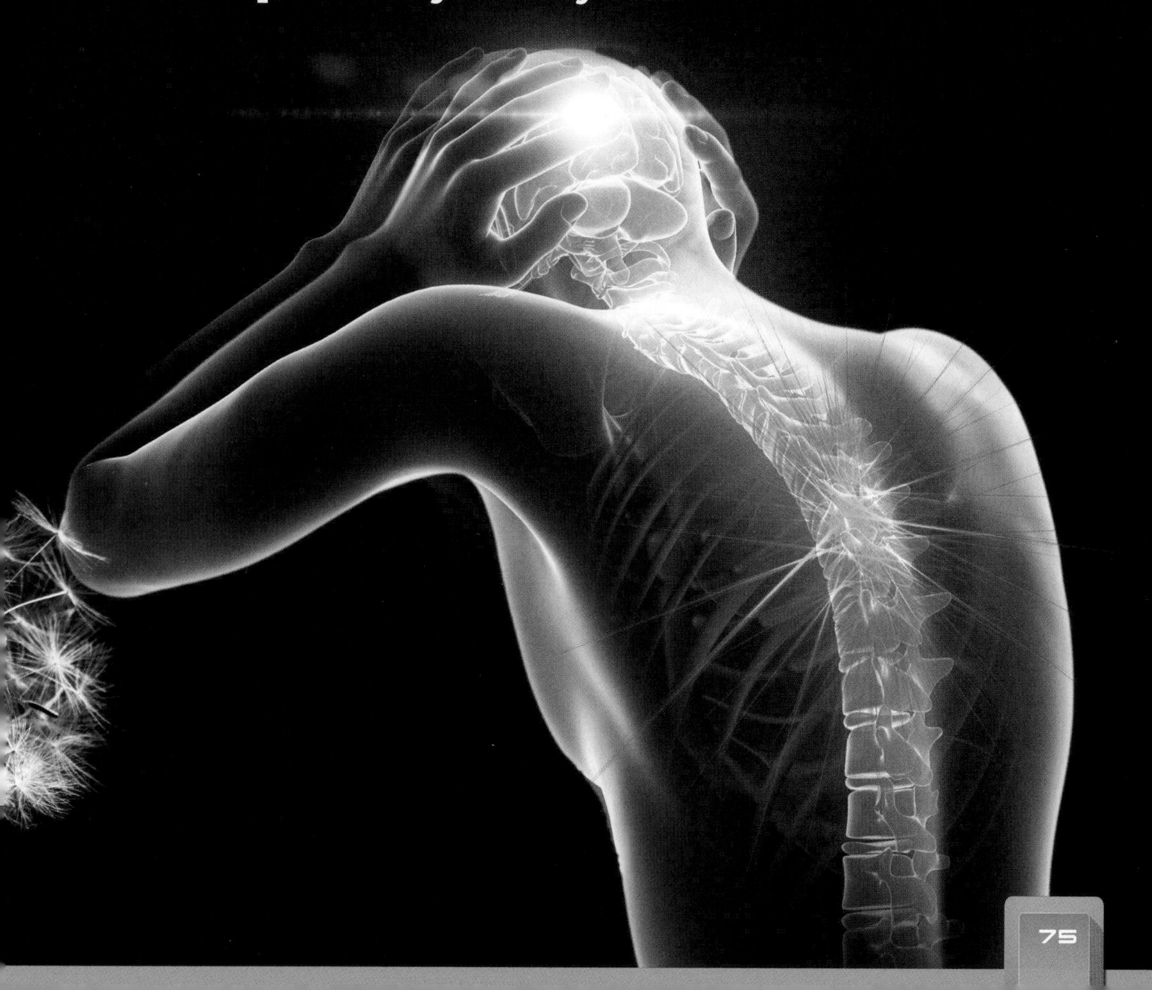

# RESEARCH PROJECTS

1. Select a body system from this book and find out more about things that can go wrong with it. What can medicine do to addre those problems?

2. Using this text and other sources, find out more about what steps people can take to limit their exposure to diseases. Make a of tips and turn it into a poster or pamphlet.

3. There are a variety of things that cause more than their share diseases, such as contaminated water, mosquitoes, and cigarette smoke. Choose one of these or some other that interests you an study the many problems it can cause. Write a report on what ought to be done in the future to limit these problems.

4. Do some research on occupational diseases. Besides the ones mentioned in the text, what are some other causes of occupational disease and injury? Find out what rights different types of workers have. Consider choosing a particular field and writing a report on the state of occupational disease and injury.

5. Find out more about the history of vaccination and how the process has changed the world. How was the process discovered? What are the most significant vaccines that have been invented? Make a timeline of key events.

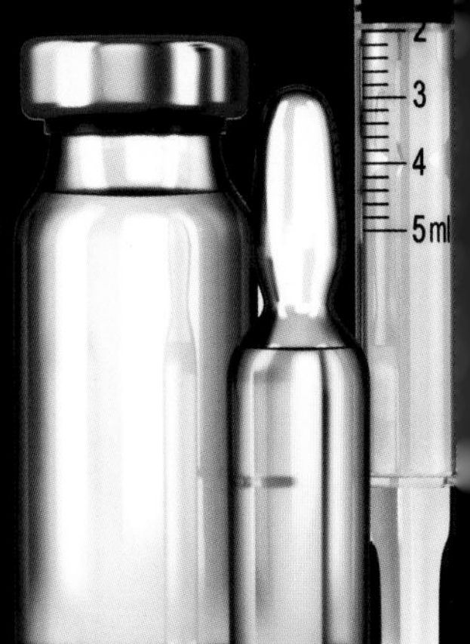

# FURTHER READING


Asselin, Kristine. *Dangerous Diseases*. North Mankato, MN: Capstone, 2014.

Bennett, Howard. *Fantastic Body: What Makes It Tick & How You Get Sick*. Emmaus, PA: Rodale, 2017.

Diamond, Jared. *Guns, Germs, and Steel*. Twentieth Anniversary Edition. New York: W.W. Norton, 2017

Gardy, Jennifer. *It's Catching: The Infectious World of Germs*. Berkeley, CA: OwlKids Books, 2014. *Human Body!* New York and London: DK Children, 2017.


# INTERNET RESOURCES

HIV/AIDS and Teens FAQ
**https://teens.webmd.com/hiv-aids-and-teens-faq#1**
This site from Web MD asks and answers many important questions about HIV/AIDS.

Outbreaks: Protecting Americans from Infectious Diseases
**http://healthyamericans.org/reports/outbreaks2015/**
A report from Trust for America's Health on epidemic preparations at the state level.

Teen Health and Wellness
**http://www.teenhealthandwellness.com/**
A comprehensive site with tons of information about the body and health.

---

# Picture Credits:

Page 5: Convit/Shutterstock.com, 6: Monkey Business Images/Shutterstock.com, 7: AYakovlev/Shutterstock.com, 8: SpeedKingz/Shutterstock.com, 9: Africa Studio/Shutterstock.com, 13: Olga Nikonova/Shutterstock.com, Photographee.eu/Shutterstock.com, 16: Muhammad Mahdi Karim, 17: Muhammad Mahdi Karim, 22: Rob Marmion/Shutterstock.com, 23: Sebastian Kaulitzki/Shutterstock.com, 24: solar22/Shutterstock.com, 25: Alexander Raths/Shutterstock.com, 26: Africa Studio/Shutterstock.com, 27: michaelheim/Shutterstock.com, 28: yodiyim/Shutterstock.com, 29: Chris Bourloton/Shutterstock.com, Sebastian Kaulitzki/Shutterstock.com, 30: Kateryna Kon/Shutterstock.com, 32: Heiko Barth/Shutterstock.com, 33: Ivana P. Nikolic/Shutterstock.com, kzww/Shutterstock.com, 37: p_ponomareva/Shutterstock.com, 38: Ocskay Bence/Shutterstock.com, 39: Goncharov_Artem/Shutterstock.com, 42: chatuphot/Shutterstock.com, 45: /Shutterstock.com, 46: Robert Kneschke/Shutterstock.com, Tefi/Shutterstock.com, 48: Eva Foreman/Shutterstock.com, 49: Africa Studio/Shutterstock.com, luna4/Shutterstock.com, 53: 02creationz/Shutterstock.com, Alexey Filatov/Shutterstock.com, 54: Evan Lorne/Shutterstock.com, 55: Tyler Olson/Shutterstock.com, 56: Elena Schweitzer/Shutterstock.com, 59: kikovic/Shutterstock.com, 60: Rokas Tenys/Shutterstock.com, 61: National Cancer Institute, 62: Billion Photos/Shutterstock.com, 69: MJTH/Shutterstock.com, 70: Rob Byron/Shutterstock.com, 71: Syda Productions/Shutterstock.com, 72: Sherry Yates Young/Shutterstock.com, ESB Professional/Shutterstock.com, 73: Watcharaporn_B/Shutterstock.com, 74: Sebastian Kaulitzki/Shutterstock.com, David Koscheck/Shutterstock.com, 75: CRYONOID Custom media/Shutterstock.com, 76: Maxx-Studio/Shutterstock.com.

# INDEX

# INDEX